James Charles Cox

Dr. James C. Cox's Exchange List of Land and Marine Shells

from Australia and the Adjacent Islands

James Charles Cox

Dr. James C. Cox's Exchange List of Land and Marine Shells
from Australia and the Adjacent Islands

ISBN/EAN: 9783337315399

Printed in Europe, USA, Canada, Australia, Japan

Cover: Foto ©Andreas Hilbeck / pixelio.de

More available books at **www.hansebooks.com**

DR. JAMES C. COX'S

EXCHANGE LIST

OF

LAND AND MARINE SHELLS

FROM

AUSTRALIA AND THE ADJACENT ISLANDS.

130 PHILLIP STREET, SYDNEY.

NEW SOUTH WALES.

———

1868.

A LIST OF SPECIES

OF

MARINE MOLLUSCA

FOUND IN

PORT JACKSON HARBOUR,

NEW SOUTH WALES,

AND ON THE ADJACENT COASTS.

CLASS CEPHALOPODA.

FAMILY OCTOPODIDÆ.

Several species of Octopus, Cistopus, Pinnoctopus, Eledone, &c., are occasionally to be met with in Port Jackson, undescribed.

FAMILY ARGONAUTIDÆ.

1. Argonauta argo. *Linn.* N.S. Wales.
2. Argonauta oryzata. *Meusch.* Coogee Bay.

Amongst the decapodous Cephalapoda, species of Loligopsis, Onychoteuthis, Loligo, Sepia, &c., occur on the coast of New South Wales, but at present they appear to be unidentified.

FAMILY AMMONIIDÆ.

3. Ammonia (Lituus) lævis. *Gray.* Bondi Bay.

CLASS GASTEROPODA.

SUBORDER PROBOSCIDIFERA.

FAMILY MURICIDÆ.

4. Murex (Pteronotus) acanthopterus. *Lam.* Watson's Bay.
5. Murex (Pteronotus) angasi. *Crosse.* Watson's Bay.
6. Murex (Chicoreus) palmiferus. *Sowerby.* Woolloomooloo Bay.

4

SUBFAMILY FUSINÆ.

7. Cantharus (Tritonidea) assimilis. *Reeve.*
   Watson's Bay.
8. Cantharus (Tritonidea) unicolor. *Angas.*
   Camp Cove.
9. Trophon hanleyi. *Angas.* Port Jackson.
10. Trophon paivæ. *Crosse.* Port Jackson.

FAMILY TRITONIIDÆ.

11. Tritonium australe. *Lam.* Vaucluse Bay.
12. Tritonium fusiforme. *Kiener.* Port
    Jackson.
13. Tritonium (Gutturnium) exaratum. *Rve.*
    Botany Bay.
14. Tritonium (Simpulum) olearium. *Linn.*
    Port Jackson.
15. Tritonium (Cabestana) spengleri. *Chemn.*
    Port Jackson Heads.
16. Tritonium (Cabestana) boltenianum.
    A. Adams. Long Bay.
17. Tritonium (Cabestana) doliarium. *Lam.*
    Coast of New South Wales.
17a. Tritonium (Epidromus) brazieri. *Angas.*
    Botany Heads.
18. Bursa (Apollon) leucostoma. *Lam.* Port
    Jackson.

FAMILY BUCCINIDÆ.

SUBFAMILY NASSINÆ.

19. Eburna (Zemira) australis. *Sowerby.*
    North Head, Port Jackson.
20. Cominella adelaidensis. *Crosse.* Middle
    Harbour.
21. Cominella filicea. *Crosse et Fisch.* Port
    Jackson.
22. Nassa (Alectrion) suturalis, var. *Lam.*
    Sow and Pigs.

23. Nassa (Alectrion) jacksoniana. *Kien.*
    Middle Harbour.
24. Nassa (Niotha) pauperata. *Lam.* Port
    Jackson.
25. Nassa (Hima) rufocincta. *A. Adams.*
    Port Jackson.
26. Nassa (Arcularia) mangeloïdes. *Reeve.*
    Port Jackson.
27. Nassa (Arcularia) labecula. *A. Adams.*
    Middle Harbour.
28. Neritula (Callomphala) lucida. *Adams*
    and *Angas.* Coogee Bay.
29. Cyllene lactea. *Adams* and *Angas.* Port
    Stephens.

SUBFAMILY PURPURINÆ.
30. Purpura (Polytropa) succincta. *Mart.*
    Port Jackson.
31. Purpura (Stramonita) neglecta. *Angas.*
    Port Jackson.
32. Purpura (Cronia) amygdala. *Kiener.*
    Port Jackson.
33. Pentadactylus(Sistrum)chaideus. *Duclos.*
    Nelson's Bay.
34. Pentadactylus (Sistrum) tuberculatus.
    De Blainville. Port Jackson.
35. Adamsia typica. *Dunker.* Port Jackson.

SUBFAMILY RAPANINÆ.
36. Rapana (Latiaxis) nodosa. *A. Adams.*
    Watson's Bay.

FAMILY DACTYLIDÆ.
37. Olivella pardalis. *Adams* and *Angas.*
    Watson's Bay.
38. Olivella leucozona *Adams* and *Angas.*
    Port Jackson.
39. Olivella nympha. *Adams* and *Angas.*
    Port Jackson.

40. Amalda marginata. *Lam.* Sow and Pigs.
41. Amalda oblonga. *Sowerby.* Port Jackson Heads.
41a. Amalda angasi. *Cox.* Broken Bay.

FAMILY VOLUTIDÆ.

42. Voluta (Scapha) magnifica. *Chemn.* Rose Bay.
42a. Voluta (Scapha) fusiformis. *Swainson.* Broken Bay.
43. Voluta (Amoria) angasi. *Sowerby.* Middle Harbour.
44. Aulica marmorata. *Swainson.* Port Stephens.

FAMILY MITRIDÆ.

45. Mitra nigra. *Chemn.* Port Jackson.
46. Mitra solida. *Reeve.* Middle Head, Port Jackson.
46a. Mitra glabra. *Swainson.* Botany Bay.
47. Mitra (Cancilla) strangei. *Angas.* Middle Harbour.

SUBFAMILY COLUMBELLINÆ.

48. Columbella versicolor. *Sowerby.* Port Jackson.
49. Columbella (Mitrella) semiconvexa. *Lam.* Watson's Bay.
50. Columbella (Mitrella) australis. *Gaskoin.* Port Jackson.
51. Columbella (Mitrella) lincolnensis. *Reeve.* Port Jackson.
52. Columbella (Mitrella) albomaculata. *Angas.* Port Jackson.
53. Columbella (Mitrella) pulla. *Gaskoin.* Port Jackson.
54. Columbella (Amycla) dermestoïdes. *Kiener.* Watson's Bay.

55. Columbella(Anachis)lentiginosa. *Hinds.*
Port Jackson.
56. Æsopus filosus. *Angas.* Port Jackson.

FAMILY MARGINELLIDÆ.

57. Marginella (Glabella) muscaria. *Lam.*
Port Jackson.
58. Marginella attenuata. *Reeve.* Port
Jackson.
59. Marginella translucida. *Sowerby.* Port
Stephens.
60. Marginella turbinata. *Sowerby.* Middle
Harbour.
61. Marginella simplex. *Reeve.* Port Jackson.
62. Marginella (Cryptospira) ovulum. *Sow.*
Port Jackson.

FAMILY CASSIDIDÆ.

63. Cassis achatina. *Lam.* Port Jackson.
64. Cassis pyrum. *Lam.* Port Jackson.

FAMILY DOLIIDÆ.

65. Dolium variegatum. *Lam.* Port Jackson.

FAMILY NATICIDÆ.

66. Natica marochiensis. *Lam.* Middle
Harbour.
67. Natica (Lunatia) plumbea. *Lam.* Middle
Harbour.
68. Natica (Lunatia) melastoma. *Swainson.*
Port Jackson.
69. Natica (Lunatia) strangei. *Reeve.* Port
Jackson.
70. Natica (Neverita) chemnitzii. *Récluz.*
Middle Harbour.
71. Natica (Neverita) lamarckiana. *Récluz.*
Port Jackson.
71a. Natica (Neverita) conica. *Lam.* Middle
Harbour.

72. Amauropsis morchi. *Adams* and *Angas.* Watson's Bay.
73. Naticina nitida. *Reeve.* Port Jackson.
74. Ruma umbilicata. *Quoy.* Port Jackson.
75. Catinus zonalis. *Quoy et Gaim.* Port Jackson.

FAMILY LAMELLARIIDÆ.
76. Lamellaria indica. *Leach.* Coogee Bay.

FAMILY SCALIDÆ.
77. Scala scalaris. *Linn.* Port Jackson.
78. Scala lineolata. *Kien.* Port Jackson.
79. Scala philippinarum. *Sowerby.* Port Jackson.
80. Scala jukesiana. *Forbes.* Port Jackson.
81. Scala (Opalia) australis. *Lam.* Port Jackson.

FAMILY PYRAMIDELLIDÆ.
82. Turbonilla nitida. *Angas.* Watson's Bay.
83. Odostomia lævis. *Angas.* Watson's Bay.
84. Odostomia lactea. *Angas.* Watson's Bay.
85. Odostomia (Parthenia) pascoei. *Angas.* Port Jackson.
86. Odostomia (Parthenia) kreffti. *Angas.* Port Jackson.
87. Styloptygma aurantiaca. *Angas.* Port Jackson.
88. Cingulina circinata. *A. Adams.* Port Jackson.

FAMILY EULIMIDÆ.
89. Eulima proxima. *Sow.* Port Jackson.
90. Eulima acicula. *Gould.* Port Jackson.
91. Mucronalia mucronata. *Sowerby.* Port Jackson.
92. Leiostraca acutissima. *Sowerby.* Port Jackson.

FAMILY ARCHITECTONICIDÆ.

93. Architectonica reevei. *Hanley.* Port Jackson.
94. Philippia lutea. *Lam.* Port Jackson.

SUBORDER TOXIFERA.

FAMILY TEREBRIDÆ.

95. Acus (Abretia) bicolor. *Angas.* Port Jackson.
96. Acus (Abretia) assimilis. *Angas.* Port Jackson.
97. Acus (Euryta) trilineata. *A. Adams* and *Angas.* Port Jackson.
97a. Ringicula australis. *Crosse.* Port Jackson.

FAMILY TURRITIDÆ.

SUBFAMILY TURRITINÆ.

98. Bela mitralis. *Adams* and *Angas.* Port Jackson.
99. Drillia (Crassispira) oweni. *Gray.* Port Jackson.
100. Drillia radula. *Hinds.* Port Jackson.
101. Drillia vexillum. *Reeve.* Middle Harbour.
102. Drillia metcalfei. *Angas.* Port Jackson.
103. Drillia coxi. *Angas.* Port Jackson.
104. Drillia beraudiana. *Crosse.* Port Jackson.
105. Drillia angasi. *Crosse.* Port Jackson.

SUBFAMILY CLATHURELLINÆ.

106. Clathurella reticosa. *Adams* and *Angas.* Middle Harbour.
107. Clathurella zonulata. *Angas.* Port Jackson.
108. Daphnella crebriplicata. *Reeve.* Port Jackson.

109. Daphnella lymnæformis. *Kiener.* Middle Harbour.
110. Cithara compta. *Adams* and *Angas.* Port Jackson.
111. Mangelia picta. *Adams* and *Angas.* Port Jackson.
112. Mangelia letourneuxiana. *Crosse.* Middle Harbour.

FAMILY CONIDÆ.

113. Conus maculosus. *Sowerby.* Watson's Bay.
114. Conus jukesi. *Reeve.* Port Jackson.
115. Conus grayi. *Reeve.* Middle Harbour.

SUBORDER ROSTRIFERA.
FAMILY CYPRÆIDÆ.

116. Cyprovula umbilicata. *Sowerby.* Port Jackson.
117. Cypræa vitellus. *Linn.* Woolloomooloo Bay.
118. Cypræa caput-serpentis. *Linn.* Manly.
118a. Cypræa caurica. *Linn.* Broken Bay.
119. Cypræa asellus. *Linn.* Long Bay.
120. Cypræa clandestina. *Linn.* Watson's Bay.
120a. Cypræa staphlæa. *Linn.* Broken Bay.
121. Cypræa carneola. *Linn.* Long Bay.
121a. Cypræa annulus. *Linn.* Vaucluse.
121b. Cypræa erosa. *Linn.* Broken Bay.
121c. Cypræa tabescens. *Solander.* Lake Macquarie.
122. Cypræa xanthodon. *Gray.* Watson's Bay.
122a. Cypræa scurra. *Chemn.* Broken Bay.
123. Cypræa errones. *Linn.* Manly Beach.
124. Cypræa felina. *Gmel.* Middle Harbour.
125. Cypræa piperata. *Gray.* Port Jackson.
126. Cypræ amacula *A. Adams.* Port Jackson.

126a. Cypræa spurca, var. *Linn.* Middle Harbour.

127. Trivia australis. *Lam.* Port Jackson.

FAMILY AMPHIPERASIDÆ.

128. Amphiperas hordacea. *Lam.* Port Jackson.

129. Volva angasi. *A. Adams.* Watson's Bay.

FAMILY STROMBIDÆ.

130. Strombus (Canarium) luhuanus. *Linn.* Vaucluse Bay.

131. Strombus (Canarium) floridus. *Lam.* Port Jackson.

FAMILY APORRHAIDÆ.

132. Pelicaria scutulata. *Martyn.* Watson's Bay.

FAMILY CANCELLARIIDÆ.

133. Cancellaria granosa. *Sowerby.* Middle Harbour.

FAMILY CERITHIIDÆ.

134. Bittium granarium. *Kiener.* Port Jackson.

135. Lampania australis. *Quoy.* Port Jackson.

136. Potamides ebeninum. *Brug.* Woolloomooloo Bay.

FAMILY CERITHIOPSIDÆ.

137. Triphoris nigrofuscus. *A. Adams.* Port Jackson.

138. Triphoris labiatus. *A. Adams.* Port Jackson.

FAMILY LITTORINIDÆ.

139. Littorina mauritiana. *Lam.* Port Jackson.

140. Tectarius pyramidalis. *Quoy.* Port Jackson.
141. Risella lutea. *Quoy et Gaim.* Port Jackson.
142. Risella plana. *Quoy et Gaim.* Port Jackson.
143. Risella nana. *Lam.* Port Jackson.
144. Fossarina patula. *Adams* and *Angas.* Watson's Bay.

FAMILY PLANAXIDÆ.

145. Planaxis (Ninea) mollis. *Sowerby.* Coogee Bay.
146. Alaba phasianella. *Angas.* Port Jackson.

FAMILY RISSOIDÆ.

147. Rissoina variegata. *Angas.* Port Jackson.
148. Rissoina turricula. *Angas.* Port Jackson.
149. Rissoina cincta. *Angas.* Port Jackson.
150. Rissoina smithi. *Angus.* Port Jackson.

FAMILY TURRITELLIDÆ.

151. Turritella (Haustator) sinuata. *Reeve.* Middle Harbour.

FAMILY VERMETIDÆ.

152. Thylacodes decussatus. *Gmel.* Port Jackson.
153. Bivonia quoyi. *A. Adams.* Port Jackson.

FAMILY CALYPTRIDÆ.

154. Trochita (Haliotidea) calyptræformis. *Lam.* Port Jackson.
155. Galerus pellucidus. *Reeve.* Port
156. Crypta (Crepipatella) aculeata. *Lam.* Port Jackson.

157. Crypta (Ianachus) unguiformis. *Lam.*
Port Jackson.

FAMILY CAPULIDÆ.

158. Cochlolepas antiquata. *Linn.* Port
Jackson.
159. Cochlolepas subrufa. *Sow.* Port Jackson.
160. Capulus violaceus. *Angas.* Long Bay.

FAMILY VANIKORIDÆ.

161. Vanikoro deshayesiana. *Recluz.* Watson's Bay.
162. Vanikoro granulata. *Recluz.* Port Jackson.
163. Vanikoro quoyana. *A.Adams.* Watson's Bay.
164. Vanikoro recluziana. *Adams* and *Angas.* Camp Cove.

ORDER SCUTIBRANCHIATA.

FAMILY NERITIDÆ.

165. Nerita (Theliostyla) atrata. *Chem.* Port Jackson.

FAMILY TROCHIDÆ.

SUBFAMILY EUTROPIINÆ.

166. Eutropia ventricosa. *Quoy et Gaim.* Middle Harbour.
167. Eutropia sanguinea. *Reeve.* Port Jackson.
168. Eutropia (Tricolia) kochii. *Phil.* Port Jackson.
169. Eutropia (Tricolia) rosea. *Angas.* Coogee Bay.
170. Eutropia (Tricolia) virgo. *Angas.* Coogee Bay.

SUBFAMILY TURBININÆ.

170a. Turbo imperialis. *Gmelin.* Watson's Bay.

170b. Turbo petholatus. *Linn.* Middle Harbour.

171. Lunella undulata. *Chemn.* Port Jackson Heads.

172. Ninella straminea. *Martyn.* Port Jackson Heads.

SUBFAMILY ASTRALIINÆ.

173. Uvanilla tentoriiformis. *Jonas.* Port Jackson.

SUBFAMILY LIOTIINÆ.

174. Liotia angasi. *Crosse.* Port Jackson.

175. Adeorbis angasi. *A. Adams.* Coogee Bay.

SUBFAMILY TROCHINÆ.

176. Clanculus maugeri. *Gray.* Outer Manly.

177. Clanculus clanguloïdes *Gray.* Watson's Bay.

178. Clanculus omalomphalus. *A. Adams.* Port Jackson.

179. Clanculus gibbosus. *A. Adams.* Port Jackson.

180. Euchelus baccatus. *Menke.* Port Jackson Heads.

181. Euchelus scabriusculus. *A. Adams* and *Angas.* Port Jackson.

182. Thalotia zebrides. *A. Adams.* Port Jackson.

183. Eutrochus scitulus. *A. Adams.* Watson's Bay.

184. Canthiridus tiberianus. *Crosse.* Coogee Bay.

185. Elenchus badius. *Wood.* Middle Harbour.

186. Elenchus apicinus. *Menke.* Port Jackson.

187. Elenchus leucostigma. *Menke.* Port Jackson.
188. Bankivia varians. *Beck.* Middle Harbour.
189. Leiopyrga picturata. *H.* and *A. Adams.* Middle Harbour.
190. Trochocochlea tæniata. *Quoy et Gaim.* Port Jackson.
191. Trochocochlea porcata. *A. Adams.* Port Jackson.
192. Trochocochlea multicarinata. *Lam.* Port Jackson Heads.
193. Trochocochlea concamerata. *Gray.* Port Jackson.
194. Minolia vitiliginea. *Menke.* Middle Harbour.
195. Minolia angulata. *A. Adams.* Port Jackson.
196. Monilea corrugata. *Koch.* Outer Manly Beach.
197. Gibbula coxi. *Angas.* Port Jackson.
198. Gibbula sulcosa. *A. Adams.* Middle Harbour.
199. Gibbula strangei. *A. Adams.* Port Jackson.
200. Gibbula picturata. *Adams* and *Angas.* Coogee Bay.

SUBFAMILY STOMATELLINÆ.

201. Stomatella imbricata. *Lam.* Port Jackson.
202. Gena strigosa. *A. •Adams.* Port Jackson.

FAMILY HALIOTIDÆ.

203. Haliotis nævosa. *Martyn.* Port Jackson.
203a. Haliotis hargravesi. *Cox.* Broken Bay.

204. Haliotis cocco-radiata. *Reeve.* Watson's Bay.

204a. Haliotis brazieri. *Angas.* Vaucluse Point.

FAMILY FISSURELLIDÆ.

205. Lucapina (Glyphis) incei. *Reeve.* Port Jackson.

206. Fissurellidæa concatenata. *Crosse* and *Fisch.* Botany Bay.

207. Fissurellidæa scutella. *Gray.* Botany Bay.

208. Fissurellidæa nigrita. *Sowerby.* Port Jackson.

209. Emarginula (Hemitoma) rugosa. *Quoy et Gaim.* Port Jackson.

210. Emarginula (Clypidina) stellata. *A. Adams.* Watson's Bay.

211. Emarginula dilecta. *A. Adams.* Middle Harbour.

212. Scutus elongatus. *Lam.* Port Jackson.

213. Tugalia ossea. *Gould.* Port Jackson Heads.

FAMILY DENTALIIDÆ.

214. Antalis erecta. *Sowerby.* Sow and Pigs.

FAMILY TECTURIDÆ.

215. Tectura jacksoniensis. *Reeve.* Port Jackson.

216. Tectura scabrilirata. *Angas.* Port Jackson.

217. Tectura stellaris. *Quoy et Gaim.* Port Jackson Heads.

218. Tectura subundulata. *Angas.* Port Jackson.

219. Tectura septiformis. *Quoy et Gaim.* Port Jackson.

FAMILY GADINIIDÆ.

220. Gadinia pentigoniostoma. *Sowerby.* Coogee Bay.
221. Gadinia conica. *Angas.* Coogee Bay.

FAMILY PATELLIDÆ.

222. Patella tramoserica. *Mart.* Port Jackson.
223. Patella costata. *Sowerby.* Coogee Bay.
224. Patella aculeata. *Reeve.* Port Jackson.
225. Patella squamifera. *Reeve.* Bondi Bay.
226. Patella pentagona. *Born.* Port Jackson Heads.

FAMILY CHITONIDÆ.

227. Lophyrus australis. *Sowerby.* Port Jackson.
228. Lophyrus concentricus. *Reeve.* Watson's Bay.
229. Lophyrus glaucus. *Gray.* Port Jackson.
230. Lophyrus muricatus. *A. Adams.* Por. Jacksont
231. Lophyrus jugosus. *Gould.* Camp Cove.
232. Lophyrus smaragdinus. *Angas.* Port Jackson.
233. Lepidopleurus proteus. *Reeve.* Port Jackson.
234. Lepidopleurus longicymba. *De Blanville.* Watson's Bay.
235. Lepidopleurus ustulatus. *Reeve.* Watson's Bay.
236. Lepidopleurus antiquus. *Reeve.* Port Jackson.
237. Tonicia carpenteri. *Angas.* Port Jackson.
238. Leptochiton versicolor. *A. Adams.* Botany Bay Heads.

239. Onithochiton incei. *Reeve.* Watson's Bay.
240. Onithochiton rugulosus. *Angas.* Port Jackson.
241. Chiton piceus. *Gmel.* Port Jackson.
242. Chætopleura rugosa. *Gray.* Port Jackson.
243. Lorica cimolia. *Reeve.* Watson's Bay.
244. Plaxiphora petholata. *Sowerby.* Port Jackson.
245. Acanthochites costatus. *H. Adams* and *Angas.* Watson's Bay.
246. Acanthochites scutiger. *Adams* and *Reeve.* Watson's Bay.
247. Acanthochites carinatus. *H. Adams* and *Angas.* Port Jackson.
248. Microplax grayi. *H. Adams* and *Angas.* Port Jackson.
249. Cryptoplax striatus. *Lam.* Port Jackson.

ORDER TECTIBRANCHIATA.

250. Buccinulus affinis. *A. Adams.* Port Jackson.
251. Myonia concinna. *A. Admas.* Port Jackson.
252. Leucotina esther. *Angas.* Port Jackson.
252a. Ringicula denticulata. *Gould.* Goat Island, Port Jackson.

FAMILY APLUSTRIDÆ.

253. Hydatina physis. *Lin.* Vaucluse Bay.
254. Bullina lineata. *Wood.* Middle Harbour.

FAMILY CYLICHNIDÆ.

255. Cylichna arachis. *Quoy.* Port Jackson.
256. Tornatina fusiformis. *A. Adams.* Port Jackson.

FAMILY BULLIDÆ.

257. Bulla oblonga. *A. Adams.* Port Jackson.
258. Bulla punctulata. *A. Adams.* Port Jackson.
259. Bulla solida. *Gmel.* Middle Harbour.
260. Bulla magdelus. *Lister.* Middle Harbour.
261. Haminia brevis. *Quoy et Gaim.* Middle Harbour.
262. Akera soluta. *Chemn.* Botany Bay.

FAMILY PHILINIDÆ.

263. Philine angasi. *Crosse.* Port Jackson.
264. Chelidonura adamsi. *Angas.* Bottle and Glass.
264a. Cylindrobulla fischeri. *Adams* and *Angas.* Lane Cove River.

FAMILY APLYSIIDÆ.

265. Dolabella scapula. *Martyn.* Parramatta River.
266. Aplysia tigrina. *Rang.* Middle Harbour.
267. Syphonata keraudreni. *Rang.* Middle Harbour.

SUBFAMILY OPERCULATINÆ.

268. Operculatum indicum. *Lam.* Botany Bay.

ORDER NUDIBRANCHIATA.

FAMILY DORIDIDÆ.

269. Doris variabilis. *Angas.* Port Jackson.
270. Doris denisoni. *Angas.* Port Jackson.
271. Doris chrysoderma. *Angas.* Port Jackson
272. Doris arbutus. *Angas.* Port Jackson.
273. Doris pantherina. *Angas.* Port Jackson.

274. Doris nodulosa. *Angas.* Port Jackson.
275. Doris carneola. *Angas.* Port Jackson.
276. Actinodoris australis. *Angas.* Port Jackson.
277. Angasiella edwardsii. *Angas.* Port Jackson.

FAMILY GONIODORIDIDÆ.

278. Goniodoris atromarginata. *Cuvier.* Port Jackson.
279. Goniodoris bennetti. *Angas.* Port Jackson.
280. Goniodoris loringi. *Angas.* Port Jackson.
281. Goniodoris festiva. *Angas.* Port Jackson.
282. Goniodoris daphne. *Angas.* Port Jackson.
283. Goniodoris crossei. *Angas.* Port Jackson.
284. Goniodoris splendida. *Angas.* Port Jackson.
285. Goniodoris verrucosa. *Crssse.* Port Jackson.
286. Goniodoris erinaceus. *Crosse.* Port Jackson.

FAMILY POLYCERIDÆ.

287. Polycera cooki. *Angas.* Port Jackson.
288. Plocamophorus imperialis. *Angas.* Port Jackson.

FAMILY TRIOPIDÆ.

289. Triopa yatesi. *Angas.* Port Jackson.

FAMILY DENDRONOTIDÆ.

290. Bornella hermanni. *Angas.* Port Jackson.

FAMILY MELIBÆIDÆ.

291. Melibæa australis. *Angas.* Port Jackson.

FAMILY PROCTONOTIDÆ.

292. Janus sanguineus. *Angas.* Port Jackson.

FAMILY ÆOLIDIDÆ.

293. Æolis foulisi. *Angas.* Port Jackson.
294. Æolis macleayi. *Angas.* Port Jackson.
295. Flabellina ianthina. *Angas.* Port Jackson.
296. Flabellina ornata. *Angas.* Port Jackson.
297. Flabellina newcombi. *Angas.* Port Jackson.

FAMILY ELYSIIDÆ.

298. Elysia coogeensis. *Angas.* Port Jackson.

FAMILY GLAUCINÆ.

299. Glaucus, sp.——? Port Jackson.

SUBCLASS HETEROPODA.

FAMILY IANTHINIDÆ.

300. Ianthina violacea. *Bolten.* Port Jackson.
301. Ianthina ianthina. *Linn.* Manly Beach.
302. Ianthina decollata. *Carp.* Bondi.
303. Ianthina (iodina) exigua. *Lam.* Port Jackson.

SUBCLASS PULMONIFERA.

FAMILY ELLOBIIDÆ.

304. Cassidula zonata. *H.* and *A. Adams.* Cook's River.

SUBFAMILY MELAMPINÆ.

305. Ophicardelus australis. *Quoy et Gaim.* Cook's River.
306. Ophicardelus sulcatus. *H.* and *A. Adams.* Port Jackson.

22

307. Ophicardelus quoyi. *H.* and *A. Adams.* Port Jackson.
308. Marinula xanthostoma. *H.* and *A. Adams.* Port Jackson.

FAMILY AMPHIBOLIDÆ.

309. Ampullarina quoyana. *Desh.* Rush-cutter's Bay.
310. Ampullarina fragilis. *Quoy et Gaim.* Parramatta River.

FAMILY SIPHONARIIDÆ.

311. Siphonaria scabra. *Reeve.* Port Jackson.
312. Siphonaria denticulata. *Quoy et Gaim.* Port Jackson.
313. Siphonaria funiculata. *Reeve.* Port Jackson.
314. Siphonaria bifurcata. *Reeve.* Port Jackson.
315. Siphonaria cochleariformis. *Reeve.* Port Jackson.
316. Siphonaria atra. *Quoy et Gaim.* Port Jackson.

CLASS CONCHIFERA.

ORDER PHOLADACEA.

FAMILY GASTROCHÆNIDÆ.

317. Byropa (Dacosta) australis. *Sow.* Port Jackson Heads.
318. Humphreyia strangei. *A. Adams.* Watson's Bay.

FAMILY SOLENIDÆ.

319. Solen sloanii. *Gray.* Middle Harbour.
320. Cultellus australis. *Dunker.* Lane Cove River.

FAMILY SAXICAVIDÆ.

321. Saxicava australis. *Lam.* Port Jackson.

FAMILY CORBULIDÆ.
322. Corbula tunicata. *Hinds.* Port Jackson.
323. Corbula nasuta. *Sow.* Port Jackson.
324. Corbula scaphoides. *Hinds.* Port Jackson.
325. Corbula zelandica. *Quoy et Gaim.* Middle Harbour.
FAMILY ANATINIDÆ.
326. Anatina creccina. *Valenciennes.* Port Jackson.
327. Anatina tasmanica. *Reeve.* Port Jackson.
328. Anatina prolongata. *Reeve.* Parramatta River.
329. Alicia angustata. *Angas.* South Head Reef.
330. Alicia elegantula. *Angas.* Watson's Bay.
331. Thracia anatinoïdes. *Reeve.* Port Jackson.
332. Thracia australica. *Reeve.* Port Jackson.
333. Thracia modesta. *Angas.* Ball's Head.
334. Neæra (Rhinomya) rugata. *A. Adams.* Sow and Pigs.
335. Theora nitida. *Gould.* Port Jackson.
336. Myodora crassa. *Stutchbury.* Middle Harbour.
337. Myodora pandoræformis. *Stutchbury.* Middle Harbour.
338. Myodora ovata. *Reeve.* Port Jackson.
339. Myodora brevis. *Stutchbury.* Lane Cove.
340. Myochama anomioides. *Stutchbury.* Sow and Pigs.
341. Myochama strangei. *A. Adams.* Inside North Head.

342. Chamostrea albida. *Lam.* Port Jackson.

ORDER VENERACEA.

FAMILY MACTRIDÆ.

343. Trigonella contraria. *Desh.* Port Jackson.
344. Trigonella luzonica. *Desh.* Middle Harbour.
345. Trigonella pusilla. *A. Adams.* Middle Harbour.
346. Spisula cretacea. *Angas.* Port Stephen.
347. Spisula corbuloides. *Desh.* Rushcutter's Bay.
348. Spisula producta. *Angas.* Johnson's Bay.

SUBFAMILY LUTRARIINÆ.

349. Lutraria dissimilis. *Desh.* Middle Harbour.
350. Standella ovalina. *Lam.* Middle Harbour.
351. Zenatia acinaces. *Quoy et Gaim.* Botany Bay.

FAMILY TELLINIDÆ.

352. Gari (Psammocola) togata. *Desh.* Port Jackson.
353. Gari malaccana. *Reeve.* Lane Cove.
354. Gari zonalis. *Lam.* Middle Harbour.
355. Gari (Amphichæna) menkeana. *Reeve.* Sow and Pigs.
356. Hiatula epidermia. *Desh.* Port Jackson.
357. Hiatula biradiata. *Wood.* Middle Harbour.
358. Hiatula florida. *Gould.* Illawarra Lake.
359. Tellina (Tellinella) deltoidalis. *Lam.* Illawarra Lake.
359a. Peronæoderma albinella. *Lam.* Broken Bay.

360. Tellina (Arcopagia) elliptica. *Sow.* Port Jackson.
361. Tellina (Macoma) subelliptica. *Sow.* Watson's Bay.
362. Tellina (Mæra) semitorta. *Sow.* Port Jackson.
363. Tellina (Angulus) ticaonica. *Desh.* Lane Cove.
364. Tellina tenuilirata. *Sow.* Sow and Pigs.
365. Tellina (Angulus) unifasciata. *Sow.* Port Jackson.
366. Tellina (Angulus) lilium. *Hanley.* Lane Cove.
367. Tellina semiplana. *Sow.* Port Jackson.
368. Tellina semifossilis. *Sow.* Johnson's Bay.

SUBFAMILY DONACINÆ.

369. Donax (Latona) deltoides. *Lam.* Outer Manly Beach.

SUBFAMILY PAPHIINÆ.

370. Donacilla elongata. *Desh.* Botany Bay.
371. Donacilla obtusa. *Crosse* and *Fischer.* Sand Spit, Middle Harbour.

FAMILY VENERIDÆ.
SUBFAMILY VENERINÆ.

372. Venus laqueata. *Sow.* Port Jackson.
373. Chione striatissima. *Sow.* Watson's Bay.
374. Chione (Circomphalus) roborata. *Hanley.* Sow and Pigs.
375. Chione (Circomphalus) calophylla. *Hanley.* Mouth of Lane Cove.
376. Chione (Circomphalus) alatus. *Reeve.* Wollongong.
376a. Chione (Circomphalus) tiara. *Dillwyn.* Sow and Pigs.

377. Chione (Timoclea) australis. *Sow.* Watson's Bay.
378. Chione (Marcia) fumigata. *Sow.* Illawarra Lake.
379. Chione (Marcia) lævigata. *Sow.* Port Jackson.
380. Callista disrupta. *Sow.* Watson's Bay.
381. Callista rutila. *Sow.* Watson's Bay.
382. Tivela undulosa, var. *Lam.* Watson's Bay.
383. Sunetta adelinæ. *Angas.* Port Jackson Heads.
384. Circe undatina. *Lam.* Spectacle Island.

SUBFAMILY DOSINIINÆ.

385. Dosinia sculpta. *Reeve.* Port Jackson.
386. Dosinia scabriuscula. *Phil.* Port Jackson.
387. Dosinia puella. *Angas.* Botany Bay.
388. Clementia moretonensis. *Deshayes.* Mossman's Bay.

SUBFAMILY TAPESINÆ.

389. Tapes inflata. *Desh.* Mouth of Lane Cove.
390. Tapes undulata, var. *Born.* Parramatta River.
391. Tapes turgida. *Lam.* Middle Harbour.
392. Rupellaria mitis. *Desh.* Botany Bay.
393. Rupellaria crenata. *Lam.* Port Jackson.

FAMILY PETRICOLIDÆ.

394. Choristodon rubiginosum. *A. Adams* and *Angas.* Watson's Bay.

FAMILY GLAUCONOMYIDÆ.

395. Glauconomya angulata. *Reeve.* Parramatta River.

FAMILY CARDIIDÆ.

396. Cardium (Papyridium) papyraceum. *Chem.* Middle Harbour.

397. Cardium (Papyridium) tenuicostatum. *Lam.* Port Jackson.

398. Cardium pulchellum. *Reeve.* Inside Port Jackson Heads.

399. Cardium australiense. *Reeve.* Broken Bay.

FAMILY CHAMIDÆ.

400. Chama spinosa. *Brod.* Port Jackson.

ORDER LUCINACEA.

FAMILY LUCINIDÆ.

401. Lucina simplex. *Reeve.* Botany Bay.

402. Lucina (Codakia) rugifera. *Reeve.* Watson's Bay.

403. Lucina (Codakia) parvula. *Gould.* Port Jackson.

404. Loripes tumida. *Reeve.* Port Jackson.

405. Loripes ovum. *Reeve.* Botany Bay.

406. Loripes icterica. *Reeve.* Botany Bay.

407. Loripes assimilis. *Angas.* Port Jackson.

FAMILY UNGULINIDÆ.

408. Mysia sphæricula. *Deshayes.* Parramatta River.

409. Mysia globulosa. *A. Adams.* Port Jackson.

410. Mysia (Felania) adamsi. *Angas.* Port Jackson.

411. Mysia (Felania) jacksonensis. *Angas.* Middle Harbour.

FAMILY LASEIDÆ.

412. Lasea scalaris. *Phil.* Port Jackson.

413. Lasea australis. *Souv.* Port Jackson.

414. Kellia rotunda. *Desh.* Port Jackson.

115. Kellia cycladiformis. *Desh.* Port Jackson.

416. Lepton adamsi. *Angas.* Port Jackson

FAMILY GALEOMMIDÆ.

417. Scintilla strangei. *Desh.* Port Jackson.
418. Scintilla anomala. *Desh.* Port Jackson.

FAMILY ASTARTIDÆ.

419. Gouldia australis. *Angas.* Port Jackson.
420. Mytilicardia excavata. *Desh.* Port Jackson.

FAMILY MYTILIDÆ.

SUBFAMILY MYTILINÆ.

421. Mytilus (Aulacomya) hirsutus. *Lam.* Port Jackson.
422. Mytilus dunkeri. *Reeve.* New South Wales.

SUBFAMILY CRENELLINÆ.

423. Crenella (Modiolaria) strigata. *Hanley.* Port Jackson.
424. Crenella (Modiolaria) barbata. *Angas.* Seven Mile Beach.
425. Perna australis. *Gray.* Port Jackson.
426. Perna glaberrima. *Dunker.* Parramatta River.

FAMILY VULSELLIDÆ.

427. Vulsella tasmanica. *Reeve.* Port Jackson.

FAMILY MODIOLARCIDÆ.

428. Modiolarca subtorta. *Dunker.* Cook's River.
429. Avicula pulchella. *Reeve.* Botany Bay.
430. Margaritifera fimbriata. *Reeve.* Middle Harbour.
431. Malleus albus. *Chem.* Broken Bay.

132. Pinna zeylanica. *Gray.* Middle Harbour.

ORDER PECTINACEÆ.

FAMILY TRIGONIIDÆ.

133. Trigonia pectinata. *Lam.* Sow and Pigs.

134. Trigonia strangei. *A. Adams.* Port Jackson Heads.

FAMILY ARCIDÆ.

SUBFAMILY ARCINÆ.

135. Barbatia fasciata. *Reeve.* Port Jackson.

136. Barbatia (Acar) pusilla. *Sow.* Watson's Bay.

437. Anomalocardia trapezia. *Desh.* Port Jackson.

SUBFAMILY AXINIINÆ.

438. Axinia holoserica. *Reeve.* Watson's Bay.

439. Axinia grayana. *Dunker.* Newcastle.

440. Axinia (Pectunculus) tenuicostatus. *Reeve.* Sow and Pigs.

FAMILY NUCULIDÆ.

441. Nucula strangei. *A. Adams.* Port Jackson.

442. Nucula consobrina. *A. Adams.* Parramatta River.

FAMILY LEDIDÆ.

443. Leda dohrni. *Hanley.* Sow and Pigs.

FAMILY PECTINIDÆ.

444. Pecten tegula. *Wood.* Port Jackson.

445. Vola fumata. *Reeve.* Lane Cove.

FAMILY RADULIDÆ.

446. Radula lima. *Linn.* Port Jackson.

446a. Radula (Mantellum) angulata. *Sow.* Port Jackson.

447. Radula (Limatula) bullata. *Born.* Watson's Bay.

FAMILY ANOMIIDÆ.

448. Placunanomia (Monia) ione. *Gray.* Port Jackson Heads.

FAMILY OSTREIDÆ.

449. Ostrea purpurea, var. of O. edulis. *Hanley.* Mud Oyster, Port Jackson.

450. Ostrea mordax. *Gould.* Rock Oyster, Port Jackson.

451. Ostrea circumsuta. *Gould.* Botany Bay.

452. Ostrea virescens. *Angas.* Watson's Bay.

CLASS BRACHIOPODA.

FAMILY TEREBRATULIDÆ.

SUBFAMILY TEREBRATULINÆ.

453. Waldheimia flavescens. *Lam.* Port Jackson.

453a. Terebratella sanguinea. *Chem.* Camp Cove.

SUBFAMILY MAGASINÆ.

454. Magas cumingi. *Davidson.* Port Jackson Heads.

455. Kraussia lamarckiana. *Davidson.* Port Jackson.

FAMILY LINGULIDÆ.

456. Lingula hians. *Swainson.* Middle Harbour.

LAND AND FRESH WATER SHELLS
OF NEW CALEDONIA.

GENUS I.—SUCCINEA. *Draparnaud.*
1. Succinea australis. *Ferussac.* Art Isl., N. C.

GENUS II.—HELIX. *Linne.*
2. H. artensis. *Souverbie.* Art Isl., N. C.
3. H. montrouzieri. *Souverbie.* Art Isl., N. C.
4. H. cabriti. *Gassies.* Art Isl., N. C.
5. H. multisulcata. *Gassies.* Art Isl., N.C.
6. II. turneri. *Pfeiffer.* New Caledonia.
7. II. astur. *Souverbie.* New Caledonia.
8. H. seisseti. *Montrouzier.* Kanala, N. C.
9. H. costulifera. *Pfeiffer.* Isl. of Pines, N. C.
10. H. pinicola. *Pfeiffer.* Isl. of Pines, N. C.
11. H. villandrei. *Gassies.* New Caledonia.
12. H. rusticula. *Gassies.* Isl. of Pines, N. C.
13. II. dispersa. *Gassies.* Isl. of Pines, N. C.
14. H. vetula. *Gassies.* Isl. of Pines., N. C.
15. H. testudinaria. *Gassies.* Forests of Balade, N. C.
16. H. lifuana. *Montaouzier.* Lifu, Loyalty Group.
17. H. lombardoi. *Montrouzier.* Jengen, N. C.
18. H. inæqualis. *Pfeiffer.* Balade, N. C.
19. II. Beraudi. *Gassies.* Forest of Balade, N. C

20. H. raynali. *Gassies.* Port-de-France, N. C.
21. H. luteolina. *Gassies.* Isl. of Pines, N.'C.'
22. H. baladensis. *Souverbie.* Balade, N. C.
23. H. dictyodes. *Pfeiffer.* Balade, N. C.
24. H. cespitoides. *Fischer.* New Caledonia.
24a. H. occlusa. *Gassies.* Port-de-France, N. C.
24b. H. rhizophorarum. *Gassies.* Port-de-France, N. C.

GENUS III.—BULIMUS. *Scopoli.*

25. B. fibratus. *Martyn.* Kanala, N. C.
26. B. edwarsianus. *Gassies.* Nekete, Pot Isl. N. C.
27. B. souvillei. *Morelet.* Sainte Marie de Balade, N. C.
28. B. alexander. *Crosse.* Kanala, N. C.
29. B. porphyrostomus. *Pfeiffer.* New Caledonia.
30. B. caledonicus. *Petit.* Art Isl., N. C.
31 B. pseudo-caledonicus. *Montrouzier.* Art Isl. and Balade, N. C.
32. B. scarabus. *Albers.* Art Isl., N. C.
33. B. bivaricosus. *Gaskoin.* New Caledonia.
34. B. stutchburyi. *Pfeiffer.* Nu Isl., N. C.
35. B. eddystonensis. *Pfeiffer.* Jengen, N. C.
36. B. janus. *Pfeiffer.* New Hebrides, N. C.
37. B. inversus. *Muller.* New Caledonia.
38. B. sinistrorsus. *Deshayes.* Art Isl., N. C.
39. B. zonulatus. *Pfeiffer.* Kanala, N. C.
40. B. souverbianus. *Gassies.* Art Isl. N. C.

41. B. blanchardianus. *Gassies.* New Caledonia.

41a. B. (Placostylus) eximius. *Albers.* New Caledonia.

41b. B. (Rhachis) castaneo-fasciatus. *Montrouzier* New Caledonia.

41c. B. (Placostylus) mariei. *Crosse.* Gatop, N.C.

41d. B. (Placostylus) insignis. *Petit.* New Caledonia.

41e. B. (Rhachis) magenii. *Gassies.* New Caledonia.

41f. B. (Placostylus) bairdii. *Reeve.* New Caledonia.

41g. B. luridus. *Pfeiffer.* New Caledonia.

GENUS PARTULA. *Ferussac.*

42. Partula caledonica. *Pfeiffer.* New Caledonia.

GENUS IV.—PUPA. *Lamarck.*

42a. P. artensis. *Montrouzier.* Art Isl., N. C.

GENUS V.—SCARABUS. *Montfort.*

43. S. chalcostomus. *Adams.* Art Isl., N. C.

44. S. leopardus. *Reeve.* Tuo, N. C.

45. S. nux. *Reeve.* Balade, N. C.

46. S. minor. *Gassies.* Tuo, N. C.

GENUS VI.—MELAMPUS. *Montfort.*

47. M. adamsianus. *Pfeiffer.* Art Isl., N. C.

48. M. australis. *Quoy et Gaimard.* Numea, N. C.

49. M. sciuri. *Lesson.* Balade, N. C.

50. M. cristatus. *Pfeiffer.* Woody Bay, N. C.

51. M. brevis. *Gassies.* Jengen, N. C.

52. M. layardi. *H.* and *A. Adams.* Art Isl., N. C.

53. M. triticeus. *Philippi.* Balade, N. C.
54. M. luteus. *Quoy et Gaimard.* Lifu, N. C.
55. M. trifasciatus. *Kuster.* Numea, N. C.
56. M. stuchburyi. *Pfeiffer.* Woody Bay, N. C.
57. M. variabilis. *Gassies.* New Caledonia.

GENUS VII.—PEDIPES. *Adanson.*

58. P. jouani. *Montrouzier.* Woody Bay, N. C.

GENUS VIII.—PLECOTREMA. *H.* and *A. Adams.*

59. P. typica. *H.* and *A. Adams.* Woody Bay, N. C.
60. P. souverbiei. *Montrouzier.* Woody Bay, N. C.

GENUS IX.—AURICULA. *Lamarck.*

61. A. subula. *Quoy et Gaimard.* Tuo, N. C.
62. A. semisculpta. *H.* and *A. Adams.* Isl. of Pines, N. C.
63. A. nucleus. *Martyn.* Isl. of Pines., N. C.
64. A. mustelina. *Deshayes.* Balade, N. C.

GENUS X.—TRUNCATELLA. *Risso.*

65. T. labiosa. *Souverbie.* Art Isl., N. C.
66. T. semicostata. *Montrouzier.* Art Isl., N. C.

GENUS XI.—CYCLOPHORUS. *Montfort.*

67. C. artense. *Montrouzier.* Art Isl., N. C.
68. C. montrouzieri. *Souverbie.* Art Isl., N. C.
69. C. bocageanum. *Gassies.* Tuo., N. C.

GENUS XII.—HELICINA. *Lamarck.*

70. H. togatula. *Morelet.* Art Isl., N. C.
71. H. littoralis. *Montrouzier.* Art Isl., N. C.
72. H. primeana. *Gassies.* Art Isl. of Pines. N. C.

GENUS XIII.—PLANORBIS. *Guettard.*

73. P. ingenuus. *Morelet.* New Caledonia.
74. P. montrouzieri. *Gassies.* Kanala, N. C.

GENUS XIV.—PHYSA. *Draparnaud.*

75. P. castanea. *Lamarck.* Kanala, N. C.
76. P. auriculata. *Gassies.* Balade, N. C.
77. P. obtusa. *Morelet.* Balade, N. C.
78. P. kanakina. *Gassies.* Balade, N. C.
79. P. tetrica. *Morelet.* Balade, N. C.
80. P. caledonica. *Morelet.* Balade, N. C.
81. P. hispida. *Morelet.* Balade. N. C.

GENUS XV.—MELANOPSIS. *Ferussac.*

82. M. variegata. *Morelet.* Kanala, N. C.
83. M. carinata. *Gassies.* Balade, N. C.
84. M. livida. *Gassies.* Balade. N. C.
85. M. aperta. *Gassies.* Jengen, N. C.
86. M. brevis. *Morelet.* Balade, N. C.
87. M. deshayesiana. *Gassies.* New Caledonia.
88. M. retoutiana. *Gassies.* New Caledonia.
89. M. frustulum. *Morelet.* Kanala, N.C.
90. M. neritoides. *Gassies.* Balade, N. C.

GENUS XVI.—MELANIA. *Lamarck.*

91. M. villosa. *Philippi.* Balade, N. C.
92. M. droueti. *Gassies.* Balade, N. C.
93. M. maurula. *Reeve.* Balade, N. C.
94. M. mageni. *Gassies.* Balade, N. C.
95. M. matheroni. *Gassies.* Balade, N. C.
95a. M. montrouzieri. *Gassies.* Art Isl., N. C.
96. M. lancea. *Lea.* Kanala, N. C.
97. M. moreleti. *Reeve.* Balade, N. C.
98. M. canalis. *Lea.* Balade, N. C.

99. M. macrospira. *Morelet.* Balade, N. C.
99a. M. aspirans. *Hinds.* Fairy Isl., N. C.

GENUS XVII.—NERITINA. *Lamarck.*

100. N. petitii. *Recluz.* Balade,   N. C.
101. N. beckii. *Recluz.* Balade,   N. C.
102. N. asperulata. *Recluz.* Isl. of Pines, N. C.
103. N. pulligera. *Linn.* Jengen, N. C.
104. N. bruguierii. *Recluz.* Balade, N. C.
105. N. canalis. *Sowerby.* Balade, N. C.
106. N. lecontei. *Recluz.* Balade,   N. C.
107. N. variegata. *Lesson.* Balade, N. C.
108. N. aquatilis. *Reeve.* Balade,   N. C.
109. N. navigatoria. *Reeve.* Art Isl., N. C.
110. N. nouletiana. *Gassies.* Art Isl., N. C.
111. N. souverbiana. *Montrouzier.* Jengen, N. C.
112. N. nucleolus. *Morelet.* Jengen, N. C.
113. N. pazi. *Gassies.* Jengen,   N. C.
114. N. subgranosa. *Recluz.* Art Isl., N. C.
115. N. obscurata. *Recluz.* Jengen, N. C.
116. N. aspersa. *Recluz.* Balade,   N. C.
117. N. rugata. *Recluz.* Balade,   N. C.
118. N. chimmoi. *Reeve.* Jengen,   N. C.
119. N. corona-australis. *Chemnitz.* Art Isl., N. C.
120. N. gagates. *Lamarck.* Art Isl., N. C.

GENUS XVIII.—NAVICELLA. *Lamarck.*

121. N. sanguisuga. *Reeve.* Balade, N. C.
122. N. affinis. *Reeve.* Jengen,   N. C.
123. N. haustrum. *Reeve.* Balade, N. C.
124. N. caledonica. *Morelet.* Balade, N. C.
125. N. hupeiana. *Gassies.* Balade, N. C.

GENUS XIX.—HYDROCENA. *Parreyss.*

126. H. diaphana. *Gassies.* Isl. of Pines, N. C.

127. H. fischeriana. *Gassies.* Balade, N C.

128. H. granum. *Pfeiffer.* Isl. of Pines, N. C.

129. H. maritima. *Montrouzier.* Art Isl., N. C.

GENUS XX.—AMPULLARIA. *Lamarck.*

130. A. ormophora. *Morelet.* New Caledonia.

GENUS XXI.—AMPHIBOLA. *Schumacher.*

131. A. avellana. *Gmelin.* Port-de-France, N. C.

GENUS XXII.—CYRENA *Lamarck.*

132. C. sublobata. *Deshayes.* Balade, N. C.

GENUS XXIII.—BATISSA. *Gray.*

133. B. tenebrosa (Cyrena.) *Hinds.* Balade, N. C.

134. B. fortis. *Prime.* New Caledonia.

135. B. elongata. *Prime.* New Caledonia.

A LIST OF

LAND SHELLS

FROM THE

SOUTH SEA ISLANDS.

GENUS HELIX. *Linnæus.*

1. H. (Geotrochus) acmella. *Pfeiffer.*
Ysabel Isl., Solomon Isls.

2. H. (Geotrochus) ambrosia. *Angas.*
Russell's Isl., Solomon Isls.

3. H. (Corasia) anadyomene. *Adams* and
Angas. Guadalcanar Isl., Solomon Isls.

4. H. (Hyalina) annatonensis. *Pfeiffer.*
Aneiteum Isl., New Hebrides Isls.

5. H. (Geotrochus) antrorsa. *Pfeiffer.* Hammond Isl., Solomon Isls.

6. H. (Corasia) aphrodite. *Pfeiffer.* San
Christoval Isl., Solomon Isls.

7. H. (Discus) apia. *Homb et Jacq.* Aneiteum Isl., New Hebrides Isls.

8. H. (Geotrochus) boivini. *Petit.* Ysabel
Isl., Solomon Isls.

9. H. (Camaena) bougainvillei. *Pfeiffer.*
Bougainville Isl., Solomon Isls.

10. H. (Geotrochus) boyeri. *Fischer et Bernardi.* Admiralty Isls.

11. H. (Discus) caecilia. *Pfeiffer.* Lord
Howe's Isl.

12. H. (Nanina) cæsia. *Pfeiffer.* Admiralty
Isls.

13. H. (Nanina) campbelli. *Gray.* Norfolk
Isl.

14. H. (Orobia) casca. *Gould.* Ovolan Isl., Fiji Isls.
15. H. (Geotrochus) catinus. *Pfeiffer.* Admiralty Isls.
16. H. (Xesta) capitanea. *Pfeiffer.* San Christoval Isl., Solomon Isls.
17. H. (Microcystis) chimmoi. *Pfeiffer.* Sunday Isl., Kermadee Isls
18. H. (Hyalina) cimex. *Pfeiffer.* Lord Howe's Isl.
19. H. (Geotrochus) cineracea. *Homb et Jacq.* Hammond Isl., Solomon Isls.
20. H. (Geotrochus) cleryi. *Recluz.* San Christoval Isl., Solomon Isls.
21. H. (Patula) complementaria. *Mousson.* Upolu Isl., Navigator's Isls.
22. H. (Trochomorpha) concentrica. *Guill.* Tonga Isl., Friendly Isls.
23. H. (Geotrochus) coniformis. *Ferussac.* Louisade Isls.
24. H. (Trochomorpha) costulosa. *Pfeiffer.* Ysabel Isl., Solomon Isls.
25. H. (Geotrochus) coxianus. *Angas.* Louisade Isls.
26. H. (Discus) cressida. *Gould.* Upolu Isl., Navigator's Isls.
27. H. (Discus) crouanii. *Le Guillou.* Solomon Isls.
28. H. (Geotrochus) crucibulum. *Pfeiffer.* Admiralty Isls.
29. H. (Orobia) cumulus. *Pfeiffer.* Admiralty Isls.
30. H. (Planispira) discordialis. *Ferussac.* New Ireland.
31. H. (Rotula) divisa. *Forbes* Louisade Isls.

32. H. (Helicostyla) dumonti. *Pfeiffer.* New Ireland.

33. H. (Geotrochus) eddystonensis. *Reeve.* Stephens Isl., Solomon Isls.

34. H. (Chloritis) erinaceus. *Pfeiffer.* New Georgia Isl., Solomon Isls.

35. H. (Geotrochus) eros. *Angas.* Ysabel Isl., Solomon Isls.

36. H. (Planispira) eustoma. *Pfeiffer.* Admiralty Isls.

37. H. (Geotrochus) eva. *Pfeiffer.* New Hebrides Isls.

38. H. (Trochomorpha) exaltata. *Pfeiffer.* Solomon Isls.

39. H. (Nanina) firmostyla. *Mousson.* Upolu Isl., Navigator's Isls.

40. H. (Geotrochus) flexilabris. *Pfeiffer.* New Georgia Isl., Solomon Isls.

41. H. (Nanina) flosculus. *Cox.* Norfolk Isl.

42. H. (Merope) fringilla. *Pfeiffer.* New Georgia Isl., Solomon Isls.

43. H. (Chloritis) gaimardi. *Desh.* New Georgia Isl., Solomon Isls.

44. H. (Geotrochus) gamelia. *Angas.* Ysabel Isl., Solomon Isls.

45. H. (Videna) gassiesi. *Pfeiffer.* Erromanga Isl., New Hebrides Isls.

46. H. (Hyalina) glaberrima. *Pf.iffer.* Solomon Isls.

47. H. (Patula) gradata. *Gould.* Tonga Isl., Friendly Isls.

48. H. (Trochomorpha) grossularia. *Pfeiffer.* New Georgia Isl., Solomon Isls.

49. H. (Geotrochus) helicinoides. *Homb et Jacq.* Solomon Isls.

50. H. (Trochomorpha) hidalgoiana. *Crosse.*
New Georgia Isl., Solomon Isls.
51. H. (Hydra) hombroni. *Pfeiffer.* Ysabel
Isl., Solomon Isls.
52. H. (Patula) hystricelloides. *Mousson.*
Upolu Isl., Navigator's Isls.
53. H. (Patula) ignava. *Pfeiffer.* Lord
Howe's Isl.
54. H. (Hadra) inornata. *Homb et Jacq.*
San Christoval Isl., Solomon Isls.
55. H. (Thalassia) insculpta. *Pfeiffer.* Norfolk Isl.
56. H. (Corasia) isabellensis. *Souverbie.*
New Georgia Isl., Solomon Isls.
57. H. (————) isis. *Ffeiffer.* Admiralty
Isls.
58. H. (Xesta) jenynsi. *Pfeiffer.* Tanna,
New Hebrides Isls.
59. H. (Xesta) keppelli. *Pfeiffer.* San
Christoval Isl. Solomon Isls.
60. H. H. (Corasia?) kermandeci. *Pfeiffer.*
Sunday Isl., Kermadee Isls.
61. (Corasia) lactiflua. *Pfeiffer.* Guadalcanar Isl., Solomon Isls.
62. H. (Geotrochus) lambei. *Pfeiffer.* New
Georgia Isl., Solomon Isls.
63 H. (Geotrochus) leinardiana. *Crosse.*
New Georgia Isl., Solomon Isls.
64. H. (Geotrochus) leucothöe. *Pfeiffer.* New
Georgia Isl., Solomon Isls.
65. H. (Thersites) louisiadensis. *Forbes.*
Ysabel Isl., Solomon Isls.
66. H. (Videna) lüdersi. *Pfeiffer.* Ovolau,
Isl., Fiji Isls.
67. H. (Videna) luteo-cornea. *Pfeiffer.*
Navigator's Isls.

68. H. (Ampelita) majuscula. *Pfeiffer.* New Ireland.
69. H. (Microcystis) margarita. *Homb et Jacq.* Vavau Isl., Friendly Isls.
70. H. (Videna) matura. *Pfeiffer.* Guadalcanar Isl., Solomon Isls.
71. H. (Trochomorpha) membranicosta. *Pfeiffer.* Solomon Isls.
72 H. (Geotrochus) meta. *Pfeiffer.* Ysabel Isl., Solomon Isls.
73. H. (Videna) meleagris. *Pfeiffer.* Guadalcanar Isl., Solomon Isls.
74. H. (Geotrochus) mendana. *Angas.* Stephen's Isl., Solomon Isls.
75. H. (Videna) merziana. *Pfeiffer.* San Christoval Isl., Soloman Isls.
76. H. (Geotrochus) migratoria. *Pfeiffer.* Guadalcanar Isl., Solomon Isls.
77. H. (Nanina) microconus. *Mousson.* Viti Levu Isl., Fiji Isls.
78. H. (Geotrochus) motacilla. *Pfeiffer.* Eddystone Isl., Solomon Isls.
79. H. (Dorcasia) murina. *Pfeiffer.* Admiralty Isls.
80. H. (Discus) multispirata. *Homb. et Jacq.* Vavau Isl., Friendly Isls.
81. H. (Videna) navigatorum. *Pfeiffer.* Navigator's Isls.
82. H. (Microcystis) nematophora. *Pfeiffer.* Solomon Isls.
83. H. (Geotrocus) nigrofasciata. *Pfeiffer.* Admiralty Isls.
84. H. (Nanina) nouleti. *Le Guillou.* Ovalau Isl., Fiji Isls.
85. H. (Erepta) novæ-hiberniæ. *Quoy.* New Georgia Isl., Solomon Isls.

86. H. (Trochomorpha) partunda. *Angas.* Russell's Isl., Solomon Isls.

87. H. (Nanina) pfeifferi. *Phil.* Kantavu Isl., Fiji Isls.

87a. H. (Leptaxis) phillipii. *Gray.* Phillip Isl., near Norfolk Isl.

88. H. (Xesta) politissima. *Pfeiffer.* Solomon Isls.

89. H. (Oxychina) pyxis. *Hinds.* New Ireland.

90. H. (Hadra) quercina. *Pfeiffer.* Admiralty Isls.

91. H. (Leptaxis) radiaria. *Pfeiffer.* Solomon Isls.

92. H. (Discus) rapida. *Pfeiffer.* Erromanga Isl. New Hebrides Isls.

93. H. (Hemiplecta) rufa. *Lesson.* New Ireland.

94. H. (Geotrochus) sachalensis. *Pfeiffer.* Admiralty Isls.

95. H. (Hemiplecta) samoa. *Jacq.* Upolu Isl., Navigator's Isls.

96. H. (Nanina) samoensis. *Mousson.* Upolu Isl., Navigator's Isls.

97. H. (Nanina) schmeltziana. *Mousson.* Upolu Isl., Navigator's Isls.

98. H. (Orpiella) scorpio. *Gould.* Fiji Isls.

99. H. (Thochomorpha) scytodes. *Pfeiffer.* Solomon Isls.

100. H. (Pomatia) sebacea. *Pfeiffer.* Admiralty Isls.

101. H. (Callicochlias) semirufa. *Albers.* Fiji Isls.

102. H. (Videna) semiconvexa. *Pfeiffer.* Solomon Isls.

103. H. (Geotrochus) singularis. *Pfeiffer*. Aneiteum Isl., New Hebrides Isls.

104. H. (Trochomorpha) solarium. *Quoy et Gaim*. Port Carteret, New Ireland.

105. H. Hemiplecta) sophiæ. *Gask*. Lord Howe's Isl.

105a. H. (Nanina) solomonis. *Guill*. Solomon Isls.

106. H. (Geotrochus) splendescens. *Cox*. Solomon Isls.

107. H. (Nanina) stoddarti. *Gray*. Phillip Isl.

108. H. (Hemiplecta) subtecta. *Pfeiffer*. San Christoval Isl., Solomon Isls.

109. H. (Patula) textrix. *Pfeiffr*. Lord Howe's Isl.

110. H. (Trochomorpha) tongana. *Quoy*. Tonga Isl., Friendly Isls.

111. H. (Videna) troilus. *Gould*. Upolu Isl., Navigator's Isls.

112. H. (Thersites) tricolor. *Pfeiffer*. San Christoval Isl. Solomon Isls.

113. H. (Nanina) tumulus. *Gould*. Fiji Isls.

114. H. (Nanina) unisulcata. *Mousson*. Viti Isl., Fiji Isls.

115. H. (Nanina) upolensis. *Mousson*. Upolu Isl. Navigator's Isls.

116. H. (Camaena) ursina. *Pfeiffer*. Admiralty Isls.

117. H. (Ammonoceras) veronica. *Pfeiffer*. Solomon Isls.

118. H. (Geotrochus) vexillaris. *Pfeiffer*. Hammond Isl., Solomon Isls

119. H. (Geotrochus) vitrea. *Ferussac*. Admiralty Isls.

120. H. (Zonites) vitensis. *Mousson.* Viti Levu Isl., Fiji Isls.
121. H. (Nanina) wisemani. *Brazier.* Norfolk Isl.
122. H. (Oxychion)woodlarkiana. *Souverbie.* Woodlark Isl.
123. H. (Geotrochus) xanthocheila. *Pfeiffer.* Bougainville Isl. Solomon Isls.
124. H. (Videna) xiphias. *Pfeiffer.* New Georgia Isl., Solomon Isls.
125. H. (————) zebiiolata. *Pfeiffer.* Lord Howe's Isl.

GENUS BULIMUS. *Scopoli.*
126. B. (————) alcantarae. *Bernardi.* Solomon Isls.
126a. B. (Placostylus) bivaricosus. *Gask.* Lord Howe's Isl.
127. B. (Placostylus) clervi. *Petit.* San Christoval Isl., Solomon Isls.
128. B. (Placostylus) colubrinus. *Pfeiffer.* Kantavu Isl., Fiji Isls.
129. B. (Eurytus) eddystonensis. *Pfeiffer.* Eddystone Isl., Solomon Isls.
130. B. (Charis) elobatus. *Gould.* Viti Isl., Fiji Isls.
131. B. (Placostylus) eximius. *Albers.* New Caledonia.
132. B. (Charis) founaki. *Homb et Jacq.* Ysabel Isl., Solomon Isls.
133. B. (Charis) fulguratus. *Jay.* Ovolau Isl., Fiji Isls.
134. B. (Placostylus) fuligineus. *Pfeiffer.* Aneiteum Isl., New Hebrides Isls.
135. B. (Amphidromus) janus. *Pfeiffer.* New Hebrides Isls.
136. B. (Placostylus) macgillivrayi. *Pfeiffer.* Gaudalcanar Isl., Solomon Isls.

137. B. (Charis) malleatus. *Jay.* Ovolau Isl., Fiji Isls.
138. B. (Aspastus) miltocheilus. *Reeve.* San Christoval Isl., Solomon Isls.
139. B. (Charis) morosus. *Gould.* Viti Isl., Fiji Isls.
140. B. (———) radiosus. *Pfeiffer.* New Hebrides Isls.
141. B. (Placostylus) solomonis. *Pfeiffer.* Aneiteum Isle., New Hebrides Isls.
142. B. (Placostylus) seemanni. *Dhorn.* Fiji Isls.
143. B. (Placostylus) strangei. *Pfeiffer.* Eddystone Isl., Solomon Isls.
144. B. (Charis) stutchburyi. *Pfeiffer.* New Georgia Isl., Solomon Isls.
145. B. (———) turneri. *Pfeiffer.* Erromanga Isl., New Hebrides Isl.
146. B. (Stenogyra) upolensis. *Mousson.* Upolu Isl., Navigator's Isls.
GENUS PARTULA. *Ferussac.*
147. Partula alabastrina. *Pfeiffer.* Solomon Isls.
148. Partula canalis. *Mousson.* Upolu Isl., Navigator's Isls.
149. Partula carteriensis. *Quoy.* Port Carteret, New Ireland.
150. Partula cinerea. *Albers.* Solomon Isls.
151. Partula conica. *Gould.* Tutuila Isl., Navigator's Isls.
152. Partula coxi. *Angas.* Ysabel Isl., Solomon Isls.
153. Partula decussatula. *Pfeiffer.* Navigator's Isls.
154. Partula dentifera. *Pfeiffer.* Solomon Isls.

155. Partula filosa. *Pfeiffer.* Navigator's Isls.
156. Partula glutinosa. *Pfeiffer.* Solomon Isls.
157. Partula gonochila. *Pfeiffer.* Navigator's Isls.
158. Partula lirata. *Mousson.* Viti Isl., Fiji Isls.
159. Partula macgillivrayi. *Pfeiffer.* Aneiteum Isl., New Hebrides Isls.
160. Partula micans. *Pfeiffer.* Solomon Isls.
161. Partula navigatoria. *Pfeiffer.* Tutuila Isl., Navigator's Isls.
162. Partula nodosa. *Pfeiffer.* Navigator's Isls.
163. Partula radiolata. *Pfeiffer.* New Ireland.
164. Partula reeveana. *Pfeiffer.* Solomon Isls.
165. Partula repanda. *Pfeiffer.* New Hebrides Isls.
166. Partula solomonis. *Pfeiffer.* Solomon Isls.
167. Partula spadicea. *Reeve.* Eddystone Isl., Solomon Isl.
168. Partula taeniata. *Mörch.* Fiji Isls.
169. Partula turneri. *Pfeiffer.* Erromanga Isl., New Hebrides Isls.
170. Partula zebrina. *Gould.* Tutuila Isl., Navigator's Isl.

GENUS PUPA. *Draparnaud.*

171. Pupa pediculus. *Shuttle.* Upolu Isl., Navigator's Isls.

172. Pupa problematica. *Mousson.* Upolu Isl., Navigator's Isls.

GENUS CŒLIAXIS. *Adams and Angas.*

173. Cœliaxis exigua. *Adams and Angas.* Solomon Isls.

GENUS VITRINA. *Draparnaud.*

174. Vitrina aurea. *Pfeiffer.* Solomon Isls.
175. Vitrina planospira. *Pfeiffer.* Solomon Isls.
176. Vitrina solomonia. *Pfeiffer.* Solomon Isls.

GENUS SIMPULOPSIS. *Shuttleworth.*

177. Simpulopsis solomonis. *Pfeiffer.* Solomon Isls.

GENUS SUCCINEA. *Draparnaud.*

178. Succinea crocata. *Gould.* Upolu Isl., Navigator's Isls.
179. Succinea modesta. *Gould.* Upolu Isls., Navigator's Isls.
180. Succinea putamen. *Gould.* Upolu Isl., Navigator's Isls.

PNEUMONOPOMA.

SUBORDER I.—OPISOPHTHALMA.

FAMILY I.—ACICULACEA.

GENUS TRUNCATELLA. *Risso.*

181. Truncatella pfeifferi. *Mart.* Erromanga Isl., New Hebrides Isls.
182. Truncatella rustica. *Mousson.* Navigator's Isls.
183. Truncatella valida. *Pfeiffer.* Aneiteum Isl., New Hebrides Isls.
184. Truncatella vitiana. *Gould.* Fiji Isls.

FAMILY II.—DIPLOMMATINACEA.

GENUS DIPLOMMATINA. *Benson.*

185. Diplommatina cantori. *Pfeiffer.* Lord Howe's Isl.

186. Diplommatina capillacea. *Pfeiffer.*
Lord Howe's Isl.

187. Diplommatina chordata. *Pfeiffer.*
Lord Howe's Isl.

188. Diplommatina macgillivrayi. *Pfeiffer.*
Lord Howe's Isl.

GENUS PALAINA. *O. Semper.*

189. Palaina coxi. *II. Adams.* Norfolk
Isl.

SUBORDER II.—ECTOPHTHALMA
FAMILY I.—CYCLOSTOMACEA.
SUB-FAMILY I.—CYCLOTEA.
GENUS CYCLOTUS. *Guilding.*

190. Cyclotus daucinus. *Pfeiffer.* Solomon
Isls.

191. Cyclotus diatretus. *Gould.* Fiji Isls.

192. Cyclotus macgillivrayi. *Pfeiffer.* Aneiteum Isl , New Hebrides Isls.

193. Cyclotus recluzianus. *Pfeiffer.* Solomon Isls.

SUB-FAMILY II.—CYCLOPHOREA.
GENUS CYCLOPHORUS. *Montfort*

194. Cyclophorus albidus. *Jacq.* Navigator's Isls.

195. Cyclophorus apiae. *Recluz.* Upolu
Isl., Navigator's Isls.

195a. Cyclophorus couderti. *Fisch et Bern.*
New Caledonia.

196. Cyclophorus fornicatus. *Pfeiffer.* New
Hebrides Isls.

197. Cyclophorus forbesianus. *Pfeiffer.*
Lord Howe's Isl.

198. Cyclophorus strigatus. *Gould.* Upolu
Isl., Navigator's Isls.

199. Cyclophorus tiara. *Gould.* Upolu Isl.,
Navigator's Isls.

200. Cyclophorus upolensis *Mousson.* Upolu Isl., Navigator's Isls.

GENUS LEPTOPOMA. *Pfeiffer.*

201. Leptopoma dohrni. *Adams* and *Angas.* New Georgia Isl., Solomon Isls.

202. Leptopoma hanleyanum. *Pfeiffer.* Admiralty Isls.

203. Leptopoma ignescens. *Pfeiffer.* New Ireland.

204. Leptopoma jacquinoti. *Pfeiffer.* Solomon Isls.

GENUS DERMATOCERA. *H.* and *A. Adams.*

205. Dermatocera vitrea. *Lesson.* Solomon Isls.

SUB-FAMILY III. PUPINEA.

GENUS PUPINA. *Vignard.*

206. Pupina aurea. *Hinds.* New Ireland.

207. Pupina grandis. *Forbes.* Louisada Isls.

208. Pupina keraudreni. *Vignard.* New Ireland.

209. Pupina moulinsiana. *Fischer et Bernard.* Woodlark Isl.

GENUS REGISTOMA. *Hasselt.*

210. Registoma complanatum. *Pease.* Erromanga, New Hebrides Isls.

211. Registoma cumingianum. *Pfeiffer.* Lord Howe's Isl.

SUBFAMILY V. CYCLOSTOMEA.

GENUS OTOPOMA. *Gray.*

212. Otopoma pygmaeum. *Sowerby.* New Ireland.

GENUS CYCLOSTOMUS. *Montfort.*

213. Cyclostomus levis. *Pfeiffer.* Solomon Isls.

214. Cyclostomus novæ-hiberniæ. *Quay.* New Ireland.

GENUS HYDROCENA. *Parreyss.*

215. Hydrocena parvula. *Mousson.* Upolu
Isl., Navigator's Isls.
216. Hydrocena solidula. *Pfeiffer.* Lord
Hood's Isl.

GENUS OMPHALOTROPIS. *Pfeiffer.*

217. Omphalotropis acutilirata. *Pfeiffer.*
New Hebrides Isls.
218. Omphalotropis annatonensis. *Pfeiffer.*
New Hebrides Isls.
219. Omphalotropis bifilabris. *Mousson.*
Upolu Isl., Navigator's Isls.
220. Omphalotropis bilirata. *Mousson.* Upolu
Isl., Navigator's Isls.
221. Omphalotropis bulimoides. *Jacq.* San
Christoval Isl., Solomon Isls.
222. Omphalotropis cerea. *Pfeiffer.* Norfolk Isl.
223. Omphalotropis conoidea. *Mousson.*
Upolu Isl., Navigator's Isls.
224. Omphalotropis exquisita. *Pfeiffer.*
Lord Howe's Isl.
225. Omphalotropis granum. *Pfeiffer.*
Isle of Pines.
226. Omphalotropis navigatorum. *Pfeiffer.*
Navigator's Isls.
227. Omphalotropis ovata. *Mousson.* Fiji
Isls.
228. Omphalotropis parva. *Mousson* Fiji
Isls.
229. Omphalotropis perforato. *Mousson.* Navi-
tor's Isls.
230. Omphalotropis rosea. *Gould.* Fiji Isls.
231. Omphalotropis vallata. *Gould.* Vavau
Isl., Friendly Isls.

232. Omphalotrophis zebriolata. *Mousson.*
Navigator's Isls.

FAMILY II.

SUBFAMILY II. HELICINEA.

GENUS HELICINA. *Lamarck.*

233. Helicina articulata. *Pfeiffer.* New
Hebrides Isls.
234. Helicina beryllina. *Gould.* Fiji Isls.
235. Helicina egregia. *Pfeiffer.* Solomon
Isls.
236. Helicina fischeriana. *Montrouzier.*
Woodlark Isl.
237. Helicina flammea. *Quoy.* Tonga Isl.,
Friendly Isls.
238. Helicina fulgora. *Gould.* Upolu Isl.,
Navigator's Isls.
239. Helicina gratiosa. *Pfeiffer.* Admiralty
Isls.
240. Helicina lens. *Lea.* Fiji Isls.
241. Helicina livida *Homb et Jacq.* Solomon
Isls.
242. Helicina louisiadensis. *Forbes.* Loui-
siade Isls.
243. Helicina macgillivrayi. *Pfeiffer.* Isl.
of Pines.
244. Helicina modesta. *Pfeiffer.* Solomon
Isls.
245. Helicina moquiniana. *Recl.* Solomon
Isls.
246. Helicina musiva. *Gould.* Upolu Isl.,
Navigator's Isls.
247. Helicina norfolkensis. *Pfeiffer.* Norfolk
Isl.
248. Helicina pallida. *Gould.* Fiji Isls.
249. Helicina pictella. *Pfeiffer.* Norfolk
Isls.

249a Helicina pisum. *Phil.* Savage Isl.

250. Helicina plicatilis. *Mousson.* Upolu Isl., Navigator's Isls.

251. Helicina rotella. *Sowerby.* New Hebrides Isls.

252. Helicina sandwichiensis, var. *Soul.* Loyalty Isls.

253. Helicina sphaeroidea. *Pfeiffer.* Loyalty Isls.

254. Helicina spinifera. *Pfeiffer.* Solomon Isls.

255. Helicina stanleyi. *Forbes.* Louisade Isls.

256. Helicina sublaevigata. *Pfeiffer.* New Hebrides Isls.

257. Helicina suavis. *Pfeiffer.* Admiralty Isls.

258. Helicina taeniata. *Quoy.* Vanikora Isl., Santa Cruz Isls.

259. Helicina vitiensis. *Mousson.* Fiji Isls.

260. Helicina zebriolata. *Pfeiffer.* Navigator's Isls.

SPECIES OF
AURICULACEA,
FOUND ON THE
AUSTRALIAN COASTS
AND AT THE
SOUTH SEA ISLANDS.

FAMILY AURICULACEA. *Blainville.*
SUBFAMILY II. MELAMPEA.
GENUS MELAMPUS. *Mortfort.*

1. Melampus (Ophicardelus) australis. *Quoy et Gaimard.* Brisbane Water, N.S.W., and Tasmania.
2. Melampus castaneus. *Mühlfield.* Tutuila Isl., Navigator's Isls.
3. Melampus (Tralia) costatus. *Quoy et Gaimard.* Port Cateret, New Ireland.
4. Melampus (Tralia) fasciatus. *Deshayes.* New Hebrides Isls.
5. Melampus luteus. *Quoy.* Louisade Isl., Solomon Isls., &c.
6. Melampus pulchellus. *Petit.* Vavau Isl., Friendly Isls.
7. Melampus (Ophicardelus) quoyi. *Adams.* Moreton Bay, Queensland.
8. Melampus sciuri. *Lesson.* Port Praslin, New Ireland.
9. Melampus (Ophicardelus) stutchburyi. *Pfeiffer.* Port Curtis, Queensland, Australia.

GENUS MARINULA. *King.*

10. Marinula cymbæformis, var. *Recluz.* Australia.
11. Marinula patula. *Lowe.* Moreton Bay, Queensland, Australia.

SUBFAMILY III.—AURICULEA.
GENUS PYTHIA. *Bolten.*

12. Pythia argenvillei. *Pfeiffer.* North Australian Coast.
13. Pythia chalcostoma. *Adams.* Ysabel Isl., Solomon Isls.
14. Pythia insularis. *Jacq.* Solomon Isls.
15. Pythia macgillivrayi. *Pfeiffer.* Aneiteum Isl., New Hebrides Isls.
16. Pythia nux. *Reeve.* San Christoval Isl., Solomon Isls.
17. Pythia ovata. *Pfeiffer.* Ysabel Isl., Solomon Isls.
18. Pythia pollex. *Hinds.* Ovolau Isl., Fiji Isls.
19. Pythia pollex, small var. *Hinds.* Sandwich Isl., New Hebrides Isls.
20. Pythia pyramidata. *Reeve.* Tutuila Isl., Navigator's Isls.
21. Pythia scarabæus. *Linn.* San Christoval Isl., Solomon Isls.
22. Pythia striata. *Reeve.* Aneiteum Isl., New Hebrides Isls.

GENUS PLECOTREMA. *H.* and *A. Adams.*

23. Plecotrema bicolor. *Pfeiffer.* Port Jackson, Sydney, N.S.W.
24. Plecotrema concinna. *H.* and *A Adams.* Moreton Bay, Queensland, Australia.
25. Plecotrema lirata. *H.* and *A. Adams.* Moreton Bay, Queensland, Australia.

GENUS CASSIDULA. *Ferussac.*

26. Cassidula angulifera. *Petit.* North-east
coast of Australia.
27. Cassidula doliolum, var. *Petit.* Sydney,
N.S.W., Australia.
28. Cassidula mioxi. *Lesson.* New Ireland.
29. Cassidula nucleus. *Martyn.* New Ireland.
30. Cassidula rugata. *Menke.* North coast
of Australia.
31. Cassidula sowerbyana. *Pfeiffer.* Moreton
Bay, Queensland.
32. Cassidula sulculosa. *Mousson.* Kantavu
Isl., Fiji Isls.
33. Cassidula zonata. *H.* and *A. Adams.*
Sydney, N.S.W., Australia.

GENUS AURICULA. *Lamarck.*

34. Auricula (Ellobium) auris judæ. *Linn.*
North-east coast of Australia.
35. Auricula (Leuconia) auricella. *Ferussac.*
Australia.
36. Auricula (Ellobium) elongata. *Parreyss.*
Fiji Isls. and Port Denison, Queensland,
Australia.
37. Auricula (Ellobium) subula. *Quoy et
Gaimard.* Port Carteret, New Ireland.
38. Auricula (Tralia) pellucida. *Cooper.*
Tasmania.

A LIST

OF THE

LAND SHELLS

OF NEW ZEALAND.

I.—GENUS HELIX. *Linnæus.*

1. H. (Discus) alpha. *Pfeiffer.* New Zealand.
2. H. (Discus) anguiculus. *Reeve.* New Zealand.
3. H. (————) antipoda. *Homb et Jacq.* New Zealand.
4. H. (————) aucklandica. *Guill.* New Zealand.
5. H. (Trochomorpha) beta. *Pfeiffer.* New Zealand.
6. H. (Discus) biconcava. *Pfeiffer.* New Zealand.
7. H. (Paryphanta) busbyi. *Gray.* New Zealand.
8. H. (Hygromia) celinde. *Gray.* New Zealand.
9. H. (Discus) chiron. *Gray.* Auckland, Zealand.
10. H. (Patula) coma. *Gray.* New Zealand.
11. H. (Zonites?) coresia. *Gray.* New Zealand.
12. H. (Hyalina) crebriflammis. *Pfeiffer.* New Zealand

13. H. (Hyalina?) decidua. *Pfeiffer.* New Zealand.
14. H. (Patula) dimorpha. *Pfeiffer.* New Zealand.
15. H. (Videna) dunniæ. *Gray.* New Zealand.
16. H. (Discus) egesta. *Gray.* New Zealand.
17. H. (Patula) epsilon. *Pfeiffer.* New Zealand.
18. H. (Nanina) erigone. *Gray.* Auckland, New Zealand.
19. H. (Discus) eta. *Pfeiffer.* New Zealand.
20. H. Patula) gamma. *Pfeiffer.* New Zealand.
21. H. (Conulus) glabriuscula. *Pfeiffer.* New Zealand.
22. H. (Xesta) granum. *Pfeiffer.* New Zealand.
23. H. (Videna) greenwoodi. *Gray.* Auckland Zealand.
24. H. (Nanina) guttula. *Pfeiffer.* New Zealand.
25. H. (Conulus) heldiana. *Pfeiffer.* New Zealand.
26. H. (———) hochstetteri. *Pfeiffer* (?) New Zealand.
26a. H. (Patula) hypopolia. *Pfeiffer.* New Zealand.
27. H. (Discus) ide. *Gray.* New Zealand.
28. H. (Patula) iota. *Pfeiffer.* New Zealand.
29. H. (Nanina) irradiata. *Gould.* New Zealand.
30. H. (Hyalina) jeffreysiana. *Pfeiffer.* New Zealand.
31. H. (Discus) kappa. *Pfeiffer.* New Zealand.

32. H. (Nanina) kivi. *Gray.* New Zealand.
33. H. (Hyalina) lambda. *Pfeiffer.* New Zealand.
34. H. (Pitys) leimonias. *Gray.* New Zealand.
35. H. (Microcystis) mariæ. *Gray.* New Zealand.
36. H. (Nanina) novæ-zealandiæ. *Gray.* New Zealand.
37. H. (Nanina) obnubila. *Reeve.* New Zealand.
38. H. (Microcystis) omega. *Pfeiffer.* New Zealand.
40. H. (———) phlogophora. *Pfeiffer.* New Zealand.
41. H. (Erepta) poecilosticta. *Pfeiffer.* New Zealand.
42. H. (Discus) portia. *Gray.* Auckland, New Zealand.
43. H. (Discus) rapida. *Pfeiffer.* New Zealand.
44. H. (Conulus) regularis. *Pfeiffer.* New Zealand.
45. H. (Tachea) reinga. *Gray.* New Zealand.
46. H. (———) sciadium. *Pfeiffer.* New Zealand.
46a. H. (———) taranaki. *Gray.* New Zealand.
47. H. (Microcystis) tullia. *Gray.* Auckland, New Zealand.
48. H. (Paryphanta) urnula. *Pfeiffer.* New Zealand.
49. H. (Patula) varicosa. *Pfeiffer.* New Zealand.

50. H. (———) venulata. *Pfeiffer.* New Zealand.
51. H. (Patula) zealandiæ. *Gray.* New Zealand.
52. H. (Discus) zeta. *Pfeiffer.* New Zealand.

II.—GENUS BULIMUS. *Scopoli.*

53. B. (———) novo-zealandicus. *Pfeiffer.* New Zealand.
54. B. (Placostylus) shongii. *Lesson.* Bay of Islands, New Zealand.

III.—GENUS TORNATELLINA. *Beck.*

55. T. (Leptinaria) novo-zealandica. *Pfeiffer.* New Zealand.

IV.—GENUS PUPA. *Draparnaud.*

56. P. (Isthmia) novo-zealandica. *Pfeiffer.* New Zealand.

V.—GENUS VITRINA. *Draparnaud.*

57. V. (Helicarion) dimidiata. *Pfeiffer.* New Zealand.
58. V. (Helicarion) zebra. *Le Guillou.* Auckland, New Zealand.

VI.—GENUS SUCCINEA. *Draparnaud.*

59. Succinea tomentosa. *Pfeiffer.* New Zealand.

PNEUMONOPOMA.
SUBORDER II.—ECTOPHTHALMA.
FAMILY I.—CYCLOSTOMACEA.
SUBFAMILY II.—CYCLOPHOREA.
I.—GENUS CYCLOPHORUS. *Montfort.*

60. Cyclophorus? lignarius. *Pfeiffer.* New Zealand.
61. Cyclophorus? cytora. *Gray.* New Zealand.

SUBFAMILY VIII.—REALIEA.

II.—GENUS REALIA. *Gray.*

62. Realia carinella. *Pfeiffer.* Drury Taupiri, New Zealand.
63. Realia hochstetteri. *Pfeiffer.* Bay of Islands, New Zealand.
64. Realia egea. *Gray.* New Zealand.
65. Realia turriculata. *Pfeiffer.* New Zealand.

IV.—GENUS HYDROCENA. *Parreyss.*

66. Hydrocena purchasi. *Pfeiffer.* Bay of Islands, New Zealand.

V —GENUS OMPHALOTROPIS. *Pfeiffer.*

67. Omphalotropis vestita. *Pfeiffer.* New Zealand.

FAMILY AURICULACEA. *Blainville.*

SUBFAMILY II.—MELAMPEA.

I.—GENUS MELAMPUS. *Montfort.*

68. Melampus (Tralia) adamsianus. *Pfeiffer.* New Zealand.
69. Melampus commodus. *H.* and *A. Adams.* New Zealand.
70. Melampus costellaris. *H.* and *A. Adams.* New Zealand.
71. Melampus (Ophicardelus) sulcatus. *H.* and *A. Adams.* New Zealand.
72. Melampus zealandicus. *H.* and *A. Adams* New Zealand.

II.—GENUS CASSIDULA. *Ferussac.*

73. Cassidula mustelina. *Deshayes.* New Zealand.

A LIST

OF

AUSTRALIAN LAND SHELLS.

FAMILY HELICIDÆ.

I.—GENUS HELIX. *Linnæus.*

1. H. (Discus) adelaidæ. *Pfeiffer.* Adelaide, S.A.

2. H. (Discus) albanensis. *Cox.* King George's Sound, W.A.

3. H. (Hyalina) albumenoidea. *Cox.* Flinder's Range, S.A.

4. H. (Vallonia) alexandræ. *Cox.* Sydney, N.S.W.

5. H. (Hydra) angasiana. *Pfeiffer.* Darling River, N.S.W.

6. H. (Camæna) appendiculata. *Pfeiffer.* Port Denison, Q.

7. H. (Galaxias) aridorum. *Cox.* Clarence River, N.S.W.

8. H. (Paryphanta) atramentaria. *Shuttleworth.* Mount Arnold, V.

9. H. (Xerophila) australis. *Menke.* Mount Eliza, Swan River, W.A.

10. H. (Helicophanta) banneri. *Macgillivray.* Cape Direction, Q.

11. H. (Discus) belli. *Cox.* Green Oakes, Sydney, N.S.W.

12. H. (Thersites) bidwilli. *Pfeiffer.* Richmond River, N.S.W.

13. H. (Camœna) bipartita. *Ferussac*. Cape York, N.A.
14. H. (Videna) bisulcata. *Pfeiffer*. Tasmania.
15. H. (Hydra) bitœniata. *Cox*. Port Agusta, S.A.
16. H. (Galaxias) blackmani. *Cox*. Warroo, Port Curtis, Q.
17. H. (Camœna) blomfieldi. *Cox*. Miriam Vale, Port Curtis, Q.
18. H. (Discus) bombycina. *Pfeiffer*. Mount Wellington, Tasmania.
19. H. (Discus) brazieri. *Cox*. Cook's River, N.S.W.
20. H. (Planispira) brevipila. *Pfeiffer*. New South Wales.
21. H. (Patula) bullacea. *Pfeiffer*. Clarence River, N.S.W.
22. H. (Patula) capillacea. *Ferussac*. Garden Island, Lane Cove, &c., N.S.W.
23. H. (Galaxias) carcharias. *Pfeiffer*. Shark's Bay, W.A.
24. H. (Hydra) cassandra. *Pfeiffer*. Lower Murray River, S.A.
25. H. (Camœna) cerata. *Cox*. Port Denison, Q.
26. H. (Xesta) circumcincta. *Cox*. Kiama, N.S.W.
27. H. (Discus) cochlidium. *Cox*. Clarence River, N.S.W.
28. H. (Patula) confusa. *Pfeiffer*. Wide Bay, Q., Richmond River, N.S.W.
29. H. (Geotrochus) conscendens. *Cox* Upper Richmond River, N.S.W.
30. H. (Pomatia) coriaria. *Pfeiffer*. Nulla Mountains, &c., N.S.W.

31. H (Galaxias) corneo-virens. *Pfeiffer*. Picton, N.S.W.
32. H. (Discus) corticicola. *Cox*. Richmond River, N.S.W.
33. H. (Campylaea) creedi. *Cox*. Cadell's Straits, N.A.
34. H. (Trochomorpha) cumulus. *Pfeiffer*. Manning River, N.S.W.
35. H. (Macrocyclis) cunninghami. *Gray*. Port Curtis, Q.
36. H. (Discus) cuprea. *Cox*. King George's Sound, W.A.
37. H. (Camaena) curtisiana. *Pfeiffer*. Port Curtis, Q.
38. H. (Vallonia) cyclostomata. *Le Guillou*. Port Curtis, Q.
39. H. (Discus) cygnea. *Benson*. Perth, W.A.
40. H. (Angasella) cyrtopleura. *Pfeiffer* Lake Torrens, S.A.
41. H. (Vallonia) delessertiana. *Le Guillou*. Isls. in Torres Straits, N.A.
42. H. (Thersites) delta. *Pfeiffer*. Drayton Range, Q.
43. H. (Discus) diemenensis. *Cox*. Tasmania.
44. H. (Tachea) dringi. *Pfeiffer*. Shark's Bay, W.A.
45. H. (Plagioptycha) duclosiana. *Ferussac*. New Holland.
46. H. (Hyalina) ductilis. *Pfeiffer*. Drayton Range, Q.
47. H. (Galaxias) dunkionsis. *Forbes*. Dunk Isl., N.A.
48. H. (Geotrochus) dupuyana. *Pfeiffer*. Ash Isl., Hunter River, N.S.W.

49. H. Galaxias) duralensis. *Cox.* Dural, Hawksbury River, N.S.W.

50. H. (Galaxias) edwardsi. *Cox.* Liverpool River, N.A.

51. H. (Hydra) evandaleana. *Pfeiffer.* Evandale, S.A.

52. H. (Galaxias) exocarpi. *Cox.* Mudgee, N.S.W.

53. H. (Pomatia) expeditionis. *Cox.* Tropical Australia.

54. H. (Helicophanta) falconari. *Reeve.* Richmond River, N.S.W.

55. H. (Hydra) flindersi. *Adams* and *Angas.* Flinders Range, S.A.

56. H. (Galaxias) forsteriana. *Pfeiffer.* Isls. on N.E. coast of Australia.

57. H. (Patula) franklandiensis. *Forbes.* Frankland Isl., Q.

58. H. (Callicochlias) fraseri. *Gray.* Clarence River, N.S.W.

59. H. (Hyalina) fricata. *Gould.* Illawarra, N.S.W.

60. H. (Geotrochus) fucata. *Pfeiffer.* Wide Bay, Q.

61. H. (Discus) funerea. *Cox.* Mudgee, N.S.W.

62. H. (Galaxias) funiculata. *Pfeiffer.* Isls. in Torres Straits, N.A.

63. H. (Geotrochus) gärtneriana. *Pfeiffer.* Port Essington, N.A.

64. H. (Patula) georgiana. *Quoy et Gaim.* King George's Sound, W.A.

65. H. (Hygromia) gilberti. *Pfeiffer.* Brisbane Water, N.S.W.

66. H (Pomatia) grayi. *Pfeiffer.* Clarence River, N.S.W.

67. H. (Pomatia) greenhilli. *Cox*. Upper
    Dawson River, Q.
68. H. (Videna) hamiltoni. *Cox*. Tasmania.
69. H. (Patula) harriettæ. *Cox*. Richmond
    River, N.S.W.
70. H. (Discus) hobarti. *Cox*. Tasmania.
71. H. (Camæna) incei. *Pfeiffer*. Port
    Curtis, Q.
72. H. (Rotula) indica. *Pfeiffer*. Moreton
    Bay, Q.
73. H. (Discus) inusta. *Cox*. Richmond
    River, N.S.W.
74. H. (Cysticopsis) irradiata. *Gould*.
    Australia.
75. H. (Discus) iuloidea. *Forbes*. Clarence
    River, N.S.W.
76. H. (Microcystis) jacksoniensis. *Gray*.
    Port Jackson, N.S.W.
77. H. (Hygromia) jervisensis. *Quoy et Gaim*.
    Botany Bay Swamps, N.S.W.
78. H. (Pomatia) læsa. *Reeve*. Wiseman's
    Ferry, N.S.W.
79. H. (Patula) lampra. *Pfeiffer*. Tasmania.
80. H. (Patula) lamproides. *Cox*. Tasmania.
81. H. (Videna) launcestonensis. *Reeve*.
    Tasmania.
82. H. (Discus) le grandi. *Cox*. Tasmania.
83. H. (Patula) leichhardti. *Cox*. N.E.
    Australia.
84. H. (Galaxias) leptogramma. *Pfeiffer*.
    Cygnet Bay, N.W.A.
85. H. (Camæna) lessoni. *Pfeiffer*. Port
    Curtis, Q.
86. H. (Ampelita) leucocheilus. *Cox*.
    Clarence River, N.S.W.

87. H. (Hydra) lincolniensis. *Pfeiffer*. Port
Lincoln, S.A.

88. H. (Discus) lirata. *Cox*. Sydney, N.S.W

89. H. (Videna) lizardensis. *Pfeiffer*. Lizard
Isl., N.A.

90. H. (Hydra) lorioliana. *Crosse*. Flinder's
Range, S.A.

91. H. (Hydra) luteo-fusca. *Cox*. Flinder's
Rangè, S.A.

92. H. (Hyalina) lyndhurstensis. *Cox*.
Sydney, N.S.W.

93. H. (Thersites) macgillivrayi. *Forbes*.
Frankland Isls., N.E. coast A.

94. H. (Galaxias) macleayi. *Cox*. Port
Curtis, Q.

95. H. (Helicophanta) maconelli. *Reeve*.
Brisbane, Q.

96. H. (Camæna) mansueta. *Pfeiffer*.
Richmond River, N.S.W.

97. H. (Pomatia) marcescens. *Cox*. Clarence
River, N.S.W.

98. H. (Discus) melbournensis. *Cox*. Mel-
bourne, V.

99. H. (Xesta) microcosmos. *Cox*. Darling
Point, N.S.W.

100. H. (Hyalina) minima. *Cox*. Tasmania.

101. H. (Callicochlias) mitchellæ. *Cox*.
Richmond River, N.S.W.

- 102. H. (Pomatia) monacha. *Pfeiffer*. Ash
Isl., Hunter River, N.S.W.

103. H. (Rhyssota) moretonensis. *Pfeiffer*.
Richmond River, N.S.W.

104. H. (Camæna) morosa. *Morelet*. Moreton
Bay, Q.

105 H (Discus) morti. *Cox* Sydney N.S.W

106. H. (Camæna) mucida. *Pfeiffer*. Percy
Isls., N.E. coast A.

107. H. (Discus) mucosa. *Cox*. Clarence
River, N.S.W.

108. H. (Macrocyclis) mühlfeldtiana. *Pfeiffer*.
Richmond River, N S.W.

109. H. (Pomatia) mulgoæ. *Cox*. Mulgoa,
Penrith, N.S.W.

110. H. (Camæna) murina. *Pfeiffer*.
Northern Australia.

111. H. (Discus) murphyi. *Cox*. Wollongong,
N S.W.

112. H. (Discus) murrayana. *Pfeiffer*.
Murray River, S.A.

113. H. (Patula) namoiensis. *Cox*. Namoi
River, N.S.W.

114. H. (Hyalina) nitida. *Müller*. Sydney,
N.S.W.

115. H. (Geotrochus) novæ-hollandiæ. *Gray*.
New South Wales.

116. H. (Discus) omicron. *Pfeiffer*. Richmond River, N.S.W.

117. H. (Trochomorpha) ophelia. *Pfeiffer*.
Cape York, N.A.

118. H. (Galaxias) pachystyla. *Pfeiffer*.
Port Curtis, Q.

119. H. (Galaxias) pachystyloides. *Cox*.
Cape York, N.A.

120. H. (Conulus) parramattensis. *Cox*.
Parramatta, N.S.W.

121. H. (Hydra) patruelis. *Adams* and
Angas. Port Lincoln, S.A.

122. H. (Conulus) penolensis. *Cox*. Penola,
S.A.

123. H. (Galaxias) perinflata. *Pfeiffer*.
MacDonnell Range, Central A.

124. H. (Discus) pexa. *Cox.* Prospect, N.S.W.

125. H. (Galaxias) plectilis. *Benson.* Swan River, W.A.

126. H. (Camœna) pliculosa. *Pfeiffer.* Drayton Range, Q.

127. H. (Geotrochus) poiretiana. *Pfeiffer.* Night Isl., N.E. coast A.

128. H. (Galaxias) pomum. *Pfeiffer.* `Port Essington, N.A.

129. H. (Planispira) porteri. *Cox.* Upper Clarence River, N.S.W.

130. H. (Galaxias) prunum. *Ferussac.* Port Essington, N.A.

131. H. (Patula) ptycomphala. *Pfeiffer.* Wide Bay, Q.

132. H. (Rhyssota) pudibunda. *Cox.* Richmond River, N.S.W.

133. H. (Microcystis) radians. *Pfeiffer.* Port Jackson, N.S.W.

134. H. (Patula) ramsayi. *Cox.* Richmond River, N.S.W.

135. H. (Discus) rapida. *Pfeiffer.* Cape York, N.A.

136. H. (Discus) retepora. *Cox.* Flinder's Range, S.A.

137. H. (Thersites) richmondiana. *Pfeiffer.* Richmond River, N.S.W.

138. H. (Xesta) rustica. *Pfeiffer.* Low Isls., Trinity Bay, N.E.A.

139. H. (Discus) saturni. *Cox.* Sydney, N.S.W.

140. H. (Pomatia) scotti. *Cox.* Wollongong, N.S.W.

141. H. (Camœna) semicastanea. *Pfeiffer.* Isls. near Cape York, N.A.

142. H. (Discus) sericatula. *Pfeiffer.*
Sydney, N.S.W.
143. H. (————) silveri. *Angas.* Eastern
Plains, South Australia.
144. H. (Camœna) similaris. *Ferussac.*
Double Bay, Sydney, N.S.W.
145. H. (Discus) similis. *Cox.* Tasmania.
146. H. (Videna) sinclairi. *Pfeiffer.* Tasmania.
147. H. (Planispira) spinei. *Cox.* Port
Curtis, Q.
148. H. (Hyalina) splendidula. *Pfeiffer.*
Moreton Bay, Q.
149. H. (Patula) strangei. *Pfeiffer.* Brisbane
Water, N.S.W.
150. H. (Patula) strangeoides. *Cox.* Moreton Bay, Q.
151. H. (Discus) stroudensis. *Cox.* Stroud,
N.S.W.
152. H. (Pomatia) stutchburyi. *Pfeiffer.*
Drayton Range, Q.
153. H. (Hyalina) subangulata. *Pfeiffer.*
Tasmania.
154. H. (Pomatia) subgranosa. *Le Guillou.*
Northern Australia.
155. H. (Discus) sublesta. *Benson.* Freemantle, W.A.
156. H. (Rhyssota) subrugata. *Pfeiffer.*
Clarence River, N.S.W.
157. H. (Hyalina) sydneyensis. *Cox.*
Sydney, N.S.W.
158. H. (Discus) tasmaniæ. *Cox.* Tasmania.
159. H. (Tachea) tescorum. *Benson.* Shark's
Bay, W.A.
160. H. (Camœna) thatcheri. *Cox.* Port
Curtis, Q.

161. H. (Galaxias) torulus. *Ferussac.* New
Holland.
162. H. (Conulus) turriculata. *Cox.* Port
Curtis, Q.
163. H. (Pomatia) victoriæ. *Cox.* Western
Port, V.
164. H. (Xesta) villaris. *Pfeiffer.* Cape
York, N.A.
165. H. (Discus) vinitincta. *Cox.* Upper
Richmond River, N.S.W.
166. H. (————) vitracea. *Ferussac.* New
Holland.
167. H. (Patula) walkeri. *Gray.* Port
Macquarie, N.S.W.
168. H. (Xesta) waterhousei. *Cox.* South
Australia.
169. H. (Patula) wellingtonensis. *Cox.*
Tasmania.
170. H. (Planispira) wesselensis. *Cox.*
Wessel Isl., N. coast of Australia.
171. H. (Conulus) wilcoxi. *Cox.* Clarence
River, N.S.W.
172. H. (Trochomorpha) yorkensis. *Pfeiffer.*
Cape York, N.A.
173. H. (Camæna) yulei. *Forbes.* Port
Molle, Q.
174. H. (Galaxias) zamiæ. *Cox.* Burdekin
River, Q.
175. H. (Discus) ziczac. *Gould.* New South
Wales.

II.—GENUS BULIMUS. *Scopoli.*

176. B. (Napæus) adelaidæ. *Adams* and
Angas. Rapid Bay, S.A.
177. B. (Caryodes) angasianus. *Pfeiffer.*
Port Lincoln, S.A.

178. B. (Liparus) atomatus. *Gray*. Ash
Isl., Huntor River, N.S.W.
179. B. (Rhabdotus) baconi. *Benson*.
Darling Range, W.A.
180. B. (Rhabdotus) bidwilli. *Cox*. Burnett
River, Q.
181. B. (Rhabdotus) bulla. *Menke*. Darling
Range, W.A.
132. B. (Caryodes) dufresni. *Leach*. Tasmania.
183. B. (Mesembrinus) dux. *Pfeiffer*. King
George's Sound, W.A.
184. B. (Rhabdotus) indutus. *Menke*.
Darling Range, W.A.
185. B. (Mesembrinus) inflatus. *Lamarck*.
New Holland.
186. B. (Rhabdotus) kingi. *Gray*. King
George's Sound, W.A.
187. B. (Napæus) lepidula. *Adams* and
Angas.   Shark's Bay, N.W.A.
188. B. (Rhabdotus) mastersi. *Cox*. Port
Lincoln, S.A.
189. B. (Rhabdotus) melo. *Quoy et Gaim*.
King George's Sound, W.A.
190. B. (Rhabdotus) onslowi. *Cox*. Dirk
Hartog's Isl., W.A.
191. B. (Napæus) pacificus. *Pfeiffer*. Port
Curtis, Q.
192. B. (Rhabdotus) rhodostoma. *Gray*.
New Holland.
193. B. (Mesembrinus) tasmanicus. *Pfeiffer*.
Tasmania.
194. B. (Opeas) tuckeri. *Pfeiffer*. Port
Curtis, Q.

III.—GENUS ACHATINELLA. *Swainson*.
195. A. (Frickolla) jacksonensis. *Cox*.
Sydney, N.S.W.

196 A (Frickella) wakefieldiæ. *Cox.*
Clarence River, N.S.W.

IV.—GENUS PUPA. *Lamarck.*

197. P. (Vertigo) australis. *Adams* and *Angas.* Rapid Bay, S.A.

198. P. (Vertigo) kingi. *Cox.* Parramatta, N.S.W.

199. P. (Vertigo) lincolnionsis. *Cox.* Port Lincoln, S.A.

200. P. (Vertigo) margarotæ. *Cox.* Wallaroo, S.A.

201. P. (Vertigo) moretonensis. *Cox.* Moreton Bay, Q.

202. P. (Vertigo) nelsoni. *Cox.* Nelson's Bay, Sydney, N.S.W.

203. P. (Vertigo) strangei. *Pfeiffer.* Sydney, &c., N.S.W.

V.—GENUS BALEA. *Prideaux.*

204. B. (Temesa) australis. *Forbes.* Warroo, Port Curtis, Q.

VI.—GENUS VITRINA. *Draparnaud.*

205. Vitrina aquila. *Cox.* Brisbane, Q.

206. Vitrina australis. *Pfeiffer.* Eastern Australia.

207. Vitrina castanea. *Pfeiffer.* Australia.

208. Vitrina freycineti. *Ferussac.* Lane Cove, Sydney, N.S.W.

209. Vitrina hyalina. *Pfeiffer.* Moreton Bay, Q.

210. Vitrina inflata. *Reeve.* Sydney, N.S.W.

211. Vitrina leucospira. *Pfeiffer.* Australia.

212. Vitrina macgillivrayi. *Cox.* Mitchell and Urara Rivers, N.S.W.

213. Vitrina mastersi. *Cox.* Kiama, N.S.W.

214. Vitrina megastoma. *Cox.* Clarence River, N.S.W.
215. Vitrina milligani. *Pfeiffer.* Tasmania.
216. Vitrina nigra. *Quoy et Gaimard.* Port Western, V.
217. Vitrina robusta. *Gould.* E. coast of Australia.
218. Vitrina strangei. *Pfeiffer.* New South Wales and Queensland.
219. Vitrina verreauxi. *Pfeiffer.* Tasmania and Queensland.
220. Vitrina virens. *Pfeiffer.* Moreton Bay, &c., Q.

VII.—GENUS SUCCINEA. *Draparnaud.*

221. Succinea aperta. *Cox.* King George's Sound, W.A.
222. Succinea arborea. *Adams* and *Angas.* Burnside, S.A.
223. Succinea australis. *Ferussac.* Tasmania and Australia.
224. Succinea eucalypti. *Cox.* New South Wales and Queensland.
225. Succinea macgillivrayi. *Cox.* Mulgoa, N.S.W.
226. Succinea menkeana. *Pfeiffer.* New Holland.
227. Succinea nortoni. *Cox.* Nepean River, N.S.W.
228. Succinea scalarina. *Pfeiffer.* King George's Sound, W.A.
229. Succinea strigata. *Pfeiffer.* Port Lincoln, S.A.
230. Succinea strigillata. *Adams* and *Angas.* Shark's Bay, N.W.A.

SECTION B.—OPERCULATA.

PNEUMONOPOMA. *Pfeiffer.*

SUBORDER I.—OPISOPHTHALMA. *Pfeiffer.*

FAMILY I.—ACICULACEA. *Pfeiffer.*

VIII.—GENUS TRUNCATELLA. *Risso.*

231. Truncatella brazieri. *Cox.* Sydney, N.S.W.

232. Truncatella ferruginea. *Cox.* Cape York, N.E.A.

233. Truncatella marginata. *Küster.* Port Lincoln, S.A.

234. Truncatella pfeifferi. *Martens.* Port Jackson, N.S.W.

235. Truncatella scalarina. *Cox.* Port Lincoln, S.A.

236. Truncatella teres. *Pfeiffer.* Trinity Bay, N.E.A.

237. Truncatella yorkensis. *Cox.* Cape York, N.A.

IX.—GENUS BLANFORDIA. *Menke?*

238. Blanfordia pyrrhostoma. *Cox.* Shark's Bay, W.A.

239. Blanfordia striatula. *Menke.* Adelaide, S.A.

X.—GENUS DIPLOMMATINA. *Benson.*

240. Diplommatina australiae. *Benson.* Mount Warren, N.E.A.

241. Diplommatina bensoni. *A. Adams.* Moreton Bay, Q.

SUBORDER II.—ECTOPHTHALMA. *Pfeiffer.*

FAMILY I.—CYCLOSTOMACEA. *Pfeiffer.*

SUBFAMILY II.—CYCLOPHOREA. *Pfeiffer.*

XI.—GENUS CYCLOPHORUS. *Montfort.*

242. Cyclophorus liricinctus. *Reeve.* W. Australia.

243. Cyclophorus orbiculatus. *Pfeiffer.* Swan River, W.A.

XII.—GENUS DERMATOCERA.

244. Dermatocera vitrea. *Lesson.* N.E. coast of Australia.

SUBFAMILY III.—PUPINEA. *Pfeiffer.*

XIII.—GENUS PUPINA. *Vignard.*

245. Pupina bilinguis. *Pfeiffer.* Cape York, N.A.
246. Pupina coxi. *Morelet.* Port Curtis, Q.
247. Pupina meridionalis. *Pfeiffer.* Port Denison, Q.
248. Pupina pfeifferi. *Dohrn.* Lizard Isl., N.E.A.
249. Pupina pineticola. *Cox.* Upper Richmond River, N.S.W.
250. Pupina planilabris. *Pfeiffer.* Port Curtis, Q.
251. Pupina robusta. *Cox.* Port Curtis, Q.
252. Pupina strangei. *Pfeiffer.* Moreton Bay, Q.
253. Pupina thomsoni. *Forbes.* Fitzroy Isl., N.E.A.
254. Pupina ventrosa. *Dohrn.* Endeavour River, N.E.A.
255. Pupina wilcoxi. *Cox.* Clarence River, N.S.W.

XIV.—GENUS CALLIA. *Gray.*

256. Callia splendens. *Dohrn.* Lizard Isl., N.E.A.

SUBFAMILY VIII.—REALIEA. *Pfeiffer.*

XV.—GENUS OMPHALOTROPIS. *Pfeiffer.*

257. Omphalotropis malleata. *Pfeiffer.* Australia.

FAMILY II.—HELICINACEA.
SUBFAMILY II.—HELICINEA. *Pfeiffer.*
XVI.—GENUS HELICINA. *Lamarck.*

258. Helicina diversicolor. *Cox.* Richmond
River, N.S.W., and Queensland.
259. Helicina draytonensis. *Pfeiffer.* Drayton
Range, Q.
260. Helicina fulgoror. *Gould.* Rocky Isl.,
N.E.A.
261. Helicina fumigata. *Sowerby.* Cape
Flattery, N.E. coast A.
262. Helicina gladstonensis. *Cox.* Port
Curtis, Q.
263. Helicina gouldiana. *Forbes.* Cape
Flattery, N.E. coast A.
264. Helicina lizardensis. *Cox.* Lizard Isl.,
N.E.A.
265. Helicina reticulata. *Pfeiffer.* Cape
York, N.E.A.
366. Helicina yorkensis. *Pfeiffer.* Cape
York, N.E.A.

A LIST

OF

AUSTRALASIAN VOLUTIDÆ.

I.—GENUS CYMBIUM. *Adanson.*

1. Cymbium georginæ. *Gray.* Moreton Bay and Swan River.
2. Cymbium umbilicatus. *Broderip.* Moreton Bay.
3. Cymbium broderipi. *Gray.* Torres' Straits, North Australia.
4. Cymbium diadema. *Broderip.* Port Essington and Swan River.
5. Cymbium miltonis. *Gray.* Swan River, Western Australia.

II.—GENUS SCAPHA. *Gray.*

6. Scapha mamilla. *Gray.* Tasmania, Kangaroo Isl., South Australia, Lake Macquarie Heads, N.S.W.
7. Scapha pulchra. *Sowerby.* North and N.E. Australia.
8. Scapha nivosa. *Lam.* Swan River, Western Australia.
9. Scapha norrisii. *Sowerby.* Nichol Bay, Western Australia.
10. Scapha rutila. *Broderip.* Rockingham Bay, N.E.A., and New Guinea.
11. Scapha deshayesii. *Reeve.* New Caledonia.
12. Scapha piperita. *Sowerby.* New Georgia, Solomon Isls.

13. Scapha magnifica. *Chemn.* Middle Harbour, Port Jackson.
14. Scapha punctata. *Swainson.* Broken Bay, outer Beach, N.S.W.
15. Scapha maria-emma. *Gray.* North-west coast of Australia.
16. Scapha fusiformis. *Swainson.* Broken Bay, N.S.W., and N. coast of Tasmania.

III.—GENUS LYRIA. *Gray.*

17. Lyria mitriformis. *Lam.* Streaky Bay, and Port Lincoln, S. Australia.
18. Lyria nucleus. *Lam.* Newcastle, N.S.W., also Norfolk Isl.
19. Lyria deliciosa. *Montrouzier.* Noumea, New Caledonia.

IV.—GENUS VOLUTELLA. *D'Orbigny.*

20. Volutella sophia. *Gray.* Port Essington, North Australia.
21. Volutella flavicans. *Gmel.* Port Essington, North Australia.
22. Volutella papillosa. *Swainson.* Encounter Bay, South Australia, and N. coast of Tasmania.
23. Volutella fulgetrum. *Broderip.* Port Lincoln and Encounter Bay, S,A.
24. Volutella rossiniana. *Bernardi.* New Caledonia.

IV.—GENUS ALCITHOE. *H.* and *A. Adams.*

25. Alcithoë pacifica. *Solander.* Auckland and Northern parts of New Zealand.
26. Alcithoë thatcheri. *McCoy.* Bampton Reef, South Pacific Ocean.
27. Alcithoë kreuslerae. *Angas.* Glenelg, South Australia.
28. Alcithoë gracilis. *Swainson.* New Zealand.

VI.—GENUS AMORIA. *Gray.*

29. Amoria undulata. *Lam.* Port Lincoln and Encounter Bay, South Australia.

30. Amoria angasi. *Sowerby.* Corner Inlet and Snake Isl., Victoria, also Tasmania.

31. Amoria exoptanda. *Sowerby.* Port Elliott, South Australia.

32. Amoria ellioti. *Sowerby.* Nichol Bay, Western Australia.

33. Amoria volva. *Chemn.* Swan River, Western Australia.

34. Amoria reticulata. *Reeve.* Western Australia.

35. Amoria turneri. *Gray.* North-east Australia.

36. Amoria prœtexta. *Reeve.* N.E. Australia.

37. Amoria maculata. *Swainson.* Port Curtis, Queen's Beach, Port Denison.

38. Amoria zebra. *Leach.* Brisbane Water, N.S. Wales.

39. Amoria lineata. *Leach.* Lake Macquarie, N.S.W., also Moreton Bay.

VII.—GENUS AULICA. *Gray.*

40. Aulica marmorata. *Swainson.* Lake Macquarie and Port Stephens.

ADDITIONS.

1. H. (Geotrochus) plagiostoma. *Pfeiffer.* Ysabel Isl., Solomon Isls.
2. H. (————) zenobia. *Pfeiffer.* San Christoval Isl., Solomon Isls.
3. Conus aplustre. *Reeve.* Bungaree Norah, Broken Bay.
4. Littorina scabra. *Linn.* Port Jackson, N.S.W.
5. Cypræa lutea. *Gronov.* Lake Macquarie, N.S.W.
6. Fossarina brazieri. *Angas.* Bottle and Glass Rocks, Port Jackson. N.S.W.
7. Crossea concinna. *Angas.* Sow and Pigs Reef, Port Jackson, N.S.W.
8. H. (Videna) planorbis. *Lesson.* Kantarvu Isl., Fiji Isls.
9. Ancillaria singulata. *Sow.* Broken Bay, N.S.W.
10. Tritonium chlorostomus. *Lam.* Botany Heads, N.S.W.

GENUS PARMELLA.. *H. Adams.*

11. Parmella planata. *H. Adams.* Fiji Isls.

EXPLANATORY NOTE.—N.S.W. for New South Wales; V. for Victoria; Q. for Queensland; S.A. for South Australia; W.A. for Western Australia; N.E.A. for North East Australia; N.A. for North Australia; N.W.A. for North West Australia; N.C. for New Caledonia.

www.ingramcontent.com/pod-product-compliance
Lightning Source LLC
Chambersburg PA
CBHW020324090426
42735CB00009B/1390